HARD CELL

Frank Cook
Matthew Wilkinson

This book is dedicated to Jacqueline, Dr Gillett,
Dr Marsh, Michaela Morgan and all those
friends who have helped me over the years.

©1998 Frank Cook and Matthew Wilkinson

Published by
The Bluecoat Press
Liverpool

Printed by
Design2Print (LLandudno)

Cover photograph by
Chris Wrigley

ISBN 1 872568 54 8

HARD CELL

Frank Cook
Matthew Wilkinson

The Bluecoat Press

When Frank approached Bluecoat Press, it was immediately obvious that he had an important story to tell. Frank and I met on numerous occasions, over many months, during which we recorded all his recollections. He has a superb memory and is a natural talker and was able to recount incidents from his past in colourful and, sometimes, horrifying detail.

In all my dealings with Frank, I have been impressed with his openness and honesty. Betweeen us, we have tried to produce a book which strives to present each episode in his life, as he saw it at the time, without excuses or self-pity.

The events in the book speak for themselves and, in the tragedy and waste of Frank's lost twenty-seven years, there are important messages to be found for everyone in society, as the issues surrounding crime and punishment affect us all.

Matthew Wilkinson

Early Memories

"Don't cry. Don't fucking cry." Dad was beating my younger brother Ronnie while me and my other brother Vincent looked on helplessly. I wanted Ronnie to stop crying, then maybe dad would leave him alone but Ronnie didn't stop and Dad's rage increased. He threw him out of the caravan and onto the road. It was the middle of winter and the temperature was well below zero. Thick fog covered the narrow Buckinghamshire lane. Ronnie lay on the road and I prayed the attack was over but Dad came out of the caravan and began to beat him around the body with an iron bar. He dragged him over to the ditch at the side of the road and pushed him under the filthy, freezing water, trying to drown him. After a while, his fury subsided and he dragged Ronnie's limp, semi-conscious body up the bank and threw it into the lorry. He was made to spend the night there as punishment. He was only seven at the time.

That beating was just one of many that my father inflicted on my brothers and my mum. At first, she had borne the brunt of his violence, but when she learned to hold back her tears during his attacks, he turned on us, in an attempt to upset her more. His temper was fiery and unpredictable at the best of times but, when he was drunk, he would go crazy for no reason at all and he was drunk a lot of the time. As I grew older, I tried to anticipate his moods and came to know how to please him and when to avoid him. I didn't want to please him to make him feel good, it was simply a matter of self-survival. But the beatings never stopped and, after one attack which left me with head injuries, he was jailed for nine months.

My father, Danny Cook, was of gypsy stock and my early years were spent in various campsites up and down the country. He was obsessed with money and often told me that a man is nothing without it. He was very hard-working and would engage in any legal or illegal ways of making cash. He pursued the archetypal gypsy trades, such as horse or scrap-metal dealing and was not averse to a bit of poaching or general thieving. Even so, we still lived in squalor and what money he did make was usually spent on drink and gambling. When we fell on hard times, he would resort to desperate measures to get money, usually prize-fighting. He was strong and extremely violent but his explosive temper meant he would burn out too quickly and these fights usually resulted in defeat. I can still remember the horrific injuries and huge financial loss he suffered but to him it was a simple gamble, a way to make money, by one of the few means he knew.

He was an untidy and dirty man and it still amazes me that my mother was ever attracted to him. She was a good-looking, working-class woman from a proud, South Yorkshire mining family who was fastidiously smart and tidy. Later in life, she was found to be mentally ill and I believe this could possibly explain why she got involved with a scumbag like my dad. She repeatedly suffered the greatest indignities and, although she coped for a while, my dad's violence and our harsh lifestyle, eventually drove her to a nervous breakdown.

As she was not a gypsy, she was regarded by the other travellers as a second-rate citizen and rejected by them. As a half gypsy, I was in an even worse position. I was mocked by the full gypsies because of my non-gypsy mother but also carried all the stigma of being a traveller, when I went into conventional society. From an early age, I knew I could never fit comfortably into to the gypsy culture.

I loved animals and would often spend hours in the fields, talking and playing with the horses. The gypsies laughed at me, as they regarded the horses as mere work machines. One of my jobs was to look after the cockerels, which I did with care and pride but, in the end, the cockerels were used to fight each other. I was made to watch as two cocks, which had been bred together, tore each other apart. I will never forget the looks of animal excitement on the faces of those watching, some of whom were only as old as me. The scene revolted me and convinced me I was not one of them.

My mother's desire for me and my brothers to attend school made her encourage my father to allow us to move into a council house in Doncaster. His imprisonment for beating me, gave her the perfect opportunity and we moved to a council estate on the outskirts of Doncaster, called Balby. Although our living conditions improved, life was still very difficult and we were subjected to all kinds of ridicule and prejudice. Chants of 'gypos' and 'rat-eaters' were common and, as my father was now a convict, we were stigmatised even more. Most of the neighbours could not understand what a polite, respectable woman like my mother was doing with someone like my dad.

After returning from prison, he found it impossible to adapt to conventional living and he went into a downward spiral of fighting, stealing and destroying everything he touched. The only thing he contributed to in the community was the crime rate. The attacks on us all increased in severity and frequency and the physical and mental anguish became unbearable. My mother was suffering badly and she became withdrawn and quiet. She had once been so proud of her appearance but now she was untidy and unkempt. When the pain became too much, she had a nervous breakdown and was admitted to a mental hospital.

It would be a lie to claim that my mother's illness, or even her early demise, upset me in any great way, as I didn't love her then and I don't feel any love for her now. In many ways, I resent her for not taking us away from my father and letting us suffer for so long. I was born in 1953, when she was sixteen, at a time when having a baby out of wedlock was a social disgrace. She often said to me that it was my fault that she had to stay with my father and that without me she would be free. She lacked the courage to leave the scant amount of stability that marriage provided and I still find it very hard to have any respect for her.

Ronnie, Vincent and myself, were taken in by a large, closely-knit, Doncaster family called the Colsons who became our foster parents. They were caring, kindly people who treated us in a way that we had never experienced before. For the first time in our lives, we were clean, well-dressed and well-fed but it was obvious to us that the Colsons regarded us as a kind of prize trophy and we were dragged round the neighbourhood and exhibited to all their friends.

"Look at the poor gypsy boys we've adopted, the poor little buggers!"

They talked about us in our presence and, even though what the people said was true, it hurt to hear it repeated constantly. I tried to fit in and learned to laugh along with everyone else but I was still very lonely and cried a lot. Sometimes, my emotions would spill out and I would become completely hysterical.

Mrs Colson was a large, motherly woman, who often used to smother us with her attentions. She had lots of grandchildren who would come to visit at the weekend. Naturally, she would make a great deal of fuss over them and, consequently, we found we were neglected when they came to stay. This led to a situation where we would be the focus of her kindness during the week, only to be consigned to second best at the weekends. This hot and cold scenario, actually became very disturbing and it would have been better if the Colsons had never been nice to us at all, rather than metering out their kindness in doses.

I was now attending school, where I was constantly teased about my father being a gypsy and a convict and was called the 'Colsons' orphan'. It was an unhappy time and, when my father reappeared, promising that if I joined him I would never have to go to school again and be able to stay up late, I was only too eager to go. He had treated me badly in the past but he was still my father and, as a child, I always believed his promises that things would get better.

Back on the road, things were just as bad as they had always been. We lived in total squalor and I was made to work very hard, even though I was only a child. The brutality started again and before long he was gambling and drinking heavily. My only salvation was that he would often leave me at the campsite for long periods of time, so I was free to do as I liked. I would go for long walks over the fields to the woods, where I would play fantasy games, or just cry because I felt very much alone. We were constantly travelling, being moved on by the police from site to site. In the winter, it was extremely cold and food was scarce and, when things got tough, violence would inevitably follow, with my father taking his frustration out on me. Around this time, he also began to sexually abuse me. I missed my mum.

As money became harder to come by, my father increasingly turned to crime as a source of income. I knew it was wrong to steal but shared his elation when one of his scams was successful, as it meant there would be food on the table and I wouldn't be beaten that night. After being arrested for stealing some metal, he drilled into me, "Frank, if you ever see a policeman, run." My first lesson in crime.

He thought nothing of disappearing for a few days, in pursuit of money or women, leaving me alone in the caravan, without any food. He felt that nature would not let me die and that somebody would always come to my assistance and, besides, he saved money by not feeding me.

One time, he had been away for days and all the other travellers had long since moved on. I knew something was wrong but I was too scared to search out help. I stayed in the caravan along the backroads of the Lincolnshire countryside with no food and no fresh water. I still thought my dad might return and sat around every day waiting for him. My hunger became so intense and I was so bored, that I ripped pieces from my dad's soiled shirt, which I chewed like gum and some I even swallowed. The only water I drank was from a filthy dyke. Weeks later, I was found by the cruelty man. He had a black uniform like a policeman and his van was the same as those driven by the police. I was taken back to Doncaster and put in a children's home where Ronnie and Vincent were already living. Looking back, the whole incident was remarkably like a prison transfer.

Stanley House

The cleanliness of the home was what struck me at first. Everything was spotless and reeked of detergent. It was overwhelming to enter such a massive building after living in a tiny caravan. There seemed to be hundreds of children's faces, peering out at me from every doorway, crack and cranny. I felt intimidated, especially after being on my own for so long. I couldn't even speak and just followed the staff around, only half-aware of what was happening to me.

A young, attractive girl, dressed in a smock and sandals, met me and exclaimed,

"Is it a boy or a girl?" My hair had grown so long, after weeks in the caravan, that it was hard to tell. Some of the staff came over and talked about me as if I wasn't there and shortly I was led off for a medical inspection.

Malnutrition, worms, scabies, lice, countless veruccahs on both feet and cuts and bruises from my Dad's beatings, made me a pathetic sight. I was taken to the bathroom, where they tried to scrub me clean. The water was changed twice and it was still swamp-like after each scrubbing. To add to my indignities, they put me into isolation, as it was thought I might infect the other children with the various visitors I had brought with me. The room was so clinical and clean, that, after being used to being so filthy, I found it impossible to relate to my new surroundings. I slept on the floor, as I was afraid to spoil the pristine sheets on the bed.

After a while, I was allowed to mix with the other children, which I found extremely traumatic. I was comfortable in the company of young girls and the female staff of the home, as I didn't see them as a threat but I could not be around boys and, not surprisingly, strongly distrusted adult men. My brothers, Vinnie and Ronnie, got on well together but I never played with them and had little to do with them. This was not because I didn't care for them – just the reverse – but my upbringing had left me unable to show my emotions, or to give or receive affection. My inability to associate with the boys in the home often spilled out into violence and I fought with most of them. Although I was only eight years old, I realised I was considerably stronger than most of the other children, with a natural aptitude for fighting. Winning fights earned me the respect I craved for but also put me on a pedestal which, in turn, brought problems. I found it very difficult to handle the attention and admiration of the other children.

On one occasion, my ability to fight helped to earn some freedom for the kids in the home. Every Saturday, we were allowed down to the local park for one hour and what a sight we looked, in our regulation clothes and closely-cropped hair, which painfully reinforced our feelings of alienation. We were a sitting target for the local kids, who knew we were from Stanley House. The first time I went to the park, I noticed that all the other kids from the home headed straight for a shelter which they all huddled into. The swings and slides seemed a more appealing prospect to me and I wasted no time in going over to them. Before long, a bunch of local lads came over, shouting abuse.

"You Stanley House wankers can't play on these swings," the biggest lad told me.

"Why not?" I asked, naively thinking there was a real reason.

"Because we say so," came the reply. I was quick to show him what I felt about this and promptly battered him. The other lads seemed to be somewhat taken aback and retreated to a safe distance, from where they shouted more abuse and began to throw bricks at the shelter. I went over and told the other kids that it was alright to play on the swings now and a few of the braver ones did venture over but most of them were still too scared. Some of them never left the shelter on our visits to the park during all the time I lived in the home. I was to meet many of my companions from the home later in life in various prisons around the country and we all agreed that this was surely no coincidence.

For the first eight years of my life, cruelty had been a daily reality. Now I was in Stanley House, I expected that things could only get better, after all I was now 'in care'. I could not have been more wrong.

The home was run by a fat, burly, masculine woman with limp, greasy hair, called Mrs McCabe. None of us liked her and she was capable of exceptional vindictiveness if she felt a child had misbehaved. She was assisted by her weak husband, who was a decent enough man but completely under her control.

Me and Mrs McCabe never got on and I was the focus of much of her malice. Her standard punishment was to lock me into the mop cupboard for hours, with no food. At first, I was frightened by the dark and the cold but after many stints there I came to love its peace and safety. I could avoid the draughts by sitting on a metal mop bucket but my arse used to hurt constantly. I would think about the countryside and birds nesting, which made me feel warm and comforted. The only way Mrs McCabe could get to me then, was by opening the door and sending me up to bed.

The regime of the home, like that of a nineteenth century workhouse, was extremely archaic by today's standards. Looking back, there was little difference between Stanley House and the prisons in which I would later be detained. Before breakfast, we had to do our daily chores like scrubbing the floors and setting the tables. Meals were eaten at long tables, with the eldest sitting at the head and everybody in the same places every day. After breakfast, we had to line up and file off to school in little groups. The formalised routines which characterised every aspect of our day, made us feel that we were constantly being punished, rather than cared for.

Even our free time was strictly monitored and we were only allowed out of the home, unsupervised, on Saturday mornings. Bedtimes were rigidly set out according to age and even if you were in the middle of a television programme, you had to go to bed. I was engrossed by the television, as we had never had one and I would engage in fantasy games, pretending and sometimes believing, that what I saw was real.

Like most children's homes, there was sexual abuse by some of the staff and the older kids. I didn't feel it was entirely right, but resigned myself to the fact that it was simply part of living in a home. Being used to avoiding my father, I managed to deter the advances of the perverted element of the staff and my handiness with my fists, meant I was never a target for the older kids. I remember a lot of homosexuality in Stanley House but many of the lads would get into bed with each other and cuddle, simply because it gave them some degree of comfort. In the morning, they would quickly get back into their own beds, knowing that if they were found by Mrs McCabe they would be in for a thrashing.

A shiny leather dog strap was Mrs McCabe's chosen instrument of physical punishment and there were many times she gave my arse a good whipping. What made it worse was that in order to use the strap, she would first have to take it off her fat, black Labrador. This normally placid animal, would then go crackers and try to bite chunks out of you. I can imagine that the sight of a small lad darting around a tiny room, trying to avoid a fat woman with a whip on one side and a slavering dog on the other, seems comical but, at the time, it was terrifying. Before a thrashing, Mrs McCabe could also be relied upon to come out with a venomous torrent of verbal abuse, no matter what you had done.

Some say that dogs come to resemble their owners and Mrs McCabe's Labrador, Montague, certainly shared many of her features. It was not just that it was fat and frankly rather ugly but it was able to appear pleasant when required, only to go crackers when she prompted it. Similarly, Mrs McCabe could act like the model matron when the authorities came around but we all knew about the dark side of her personality. On these rare occasions when she did treat us well, we would naively behave perfectly, hoping that by helping her impress the authorities, we would get into her good books. We should have known that it was only a front and things always reverted to normal straight away.

I recall one occasion when I was on the receiving end of Mrs McCabe's twisted sense of discipline. Sometimes, the dinners we were served were so disgusting that many of the children, especially the younger ones, were unable to eat them but if we didn't eat every bit of food on our plates, we knew we would be severely punished. I was at the head of one of the tables which had a drawer at the end of it and in a clandestine operation, the other kids would pass the horrible bits of food down to me and I would shove them into the drawer. The scheme was successful for a few weeks but, unfortunately, one of the staff checked the drawer and found the stash. When I returned from school I was called into Mrs McCabe's office where she presented me with a plate of the food I had stored in the drawer. As I was the head of the table, the blame was placed squarely on my shoulders and the matron's barbaric punishment was to make me eat all the food, some of which had been there for weeks and was rotten and covered in mould. This was to replace my evening meal, so I tried to eat some of it but passed most of it to my friends or stored it in my pockets. I managed about a third of it before vomiting on the floor. I tried to leave the room, but before I could get out, Mrs McCabe attacked me with a heavy chrome ladle, whacking me about the body and injuring one of my knees. She made me empty my pockets and eat every last piece of the filthy food.

Most of the other staff were young women and, on the whole, they didn't treat us too badly. At night, when Mrs McCabe went home, they would bring their boyfriends round and get up to all sorts in the staff quarters, which were strangely always much warmer than the rest of the home. Most kids wouldn't dare to go down, even to ask to go to the toilet. Consequently, beds were often wet, which meant trouble from Mrs McCabe in the morning. For these young girls it was only a job but they were dealing with human beings, who desperately needed their care and attention. Three sets of staff were sacked while I was there, mainly for various forms of abuse, and Mrs McCabe was sacked for malpractice after I left.

After two years in the home, I was finally considered sufficiently adjusted to attend the local school, Oswin Avenue. Because I had lived on gypsy camps until the age of eight, I had missed the majority of my primary schooling and so I was put into the bottom set. The set, known as the 'dunces class', comprised maladjusted children, immigrant Asian kids who couldn't speak English and the usual odds and sods who couldn't be fitted into the normal framework of the education system. I was more intelligent than the other members of the set and willing to learn but, as I couldn't read or write, the lessons were of no benefit to me. School offered me little stimulation and I turned to mischief, both in and out of school, to amuse myself and the other members of the class. Incidents, including lobbing paving slabs over motorway bridges, setting farm animals loose and, on one occasion, herding a sheep into the local hospital, secured my popularity with the pupils but amongst the teachers I built up a reputation as a bit of a trouble-maker.

At first, I had no qualms about being labelled in this way but I was soon to find out that it could get me into all sorts of problems. I had been sent out of a lesson for mucking about and was standing in the corridor on my own when a teacher came up and asked me if I knew anything about a stolen book. The book was about birds and I was asked whether I had seen it. Trying to be helpful, I told him that my dad had a book about birds but it was not the one they were looking for. Knowing my reputation and that my father was a gypsy, it was immediately assumed that I had stolen the book but, as I knew I hadn't, I innocently presumed they would find the culprit and thought nothing more about it.

The assembly the next day was taken by the headmaster, Mr Ibbetson, who started to talk about how he would not tolerate any thieving, swearing and stealing in his school and how he was going to make an example of someone. Then I heard,

"Will Frank Cook, of Set Seven, Year One, come up onto the stage?" I hadn't really been listening but thought that it was all a bit strange because, after all, I hadn't stolen the book. When I got onto the stage he grabbed me by the collar and started swinging me about.

"This thieving little so and so must learn his lesson," he told the whole school, who were captivated by the incident.

"Bend down," he ordered, as he slowly and deliberately pulled out his cane, treating the whole episode like a piece of theatre. He roughly pinned my head down with one hand and, with the other, gave me six of the best. My arse was absolutely killing me but I couldn't allow myself to cry, or I would lose the respect I had managed to build up amongst the other lads. When the doors opened after the assembly, I allowed myself a few tears, as I tentatively felt my tender backside. Even now, I can picture Mr Ibbetson's face as he caned me and the cruelty and malice it exuded still disturbs me. Caning was commonplace in those days, but it was still a frightening and confusing experience, which obviously did not help my already fragile trust in those in positions of responsibility.

I was making no progress in school and the teachers told me how useless I was so often that I believed them. I badly wanted to be respected and so I did what I was good at – fighting. I fought anybody I could and invariably won. This built up my reputation and I became popular with all the kids, or at least those who I didn't fight. At the same time, I was beginning to fall in with an older crowd of lads who were mostly the school's 'difficult' element and, later in life, I met a lot of them in the prison system. Being the youngest, I was lowest in the pecking order and would generally do what the other lads said. One of them, Mick Cook, also lived in Stanley House and my willingness to follow his lead, was to bring me my first taste of crime.

It happened on a Sunday, when the whole of Stanley House would go to St John's church in Balby, to attend Sunday School. We would all troop off in our clumpy, secondhand shoes, grey socks and blue anoraks, that were either too small or too large, to allow for 'growing room'. Neither me, nor Mick, was religious and so we would slope off before we got there and enjoy some freedom for an hour, while the class lasted. We were all encouraged to tell tales on one another if someone misbehaved but the kids knew that me and

12

Mick would beat them up if they dared. We also pocketed the three pence that everyone was given to put in the collection and spent it on bubblegum. One week, Mick noticed a bike, propped up outside the church and we went over to look at it more closely. He was building a bike in a local scrapyard and he needed some wheels to complete the project. He was going to let me ride on it, so I didn't think twice about helping him pinch them. Within a few seconds, he had the wheels off and now all we had to do was wait around, until it was time to go back to the home.

As we arrived back at the home, we noticed a policeman in the drive, along with Mrs McCabe and all the staff.

"Where have you two been?" the matron asked us, sternly.

"Sunday school," we both lied, simultaneously.

"Where did you get the wheels from?" Mick had told me to say that I found them on a tip, so that was exactly what I did. Not surprisingly, nobody believed me and I began to notice that I was suddenly becoming the focal point of the whole incident. I was looking to the older lad, Mick, to help me out but he seemed quite happy to let me face the music alone.

"Did Frank find the wheels on a tip?" they asked Mick.

"Yes," he replied.

"Frank, did Michael steal the wheels?" Mick was glaring at me and I knew I couldn't grass him up.

"I told you, I found them on a tip."

"Well, if you're not going to confess, we'll just have to prosecute you, for receiving two stolen bike wheels," the policeman told me. He took down my details and told me I would have to appear in a juvenile court. This didn't seem too daunting a prospect; the immediate worry was how severe the punishment Mrs McCabe was about to dish out was going to be.

Life went on as usual, in the time leading up to my court hearing and I didn't expect it would lead to much anyway. School was still boring and in the lunch breaks, a lot of us would go down to the nearby railway shunting station and muck about in the disused trains. To us, it was just a bit of an adventure but British Rail were having a crackdown on this sort of thing, as there had been some accidents and we were caught and accused of trespassing. It was all a big joke, until we were told we would have to go to the juvenile court, where I would now be charged with two offences.

The day of the trial came and I stood in court listening to my own psychiatric analysis. Dr Mather's report was full of technical jargon and the magistrates, who were mainly working-class men, asked him to explain himself in more common English.

"Young Cook is very similar to an Alsatian puppy. That is to say, he is strong, robust and susceptible to aggression. However, he is intelligent and has a lot of potential for training. But, at this point in time, he is easily led and could easily fall into a life of crime."

Looking back, I suppose the things he said were pretty accurate but to liken me to a dog was deeply upsetting and something that has stayed with me for a long time.

It was thought at the time, that if your father was a criminal, it was very likely that you would also become one. The magistrates said that in the light of my father's record, a custodial sentence must be implemented, in an attempt to correct me before I followed in his footsteps. All the other children got off, but I was given three years in an approved school.

While a place at an approved school was being found for me, I had to live in a remand home. It was an unhappy time and I quickly became sullen and introverted. I spent my time thinking about my life and the situation I now found myself in and quickly sank into depression. The term 'approved school' frightened me and I had visions of a place with a harsh regime where you were not even allowed to speak. I had no control over the direction of my life and my future looked bleak.

Dobroyd Castle

Dobroyd Castle in Todmorden was a large, old, scruffy building but that did not detract from the pervading sense of warmth and friendliness that I found there. In winter, the building would become covered in ice and, because it was floodlit, appeared to be made from glittering glass. I remember standing in the fields near the castle, very conscious of its beauty and tranquillity. The food was wholesome and plentiful and my house master and mistress, Mr and Mrs Cayton, treated me with care and affection. Despite all this, I mixed with crooks whilst I was there and, inevitably, became like them.

The first thing I noticed on arriving at Dobroyd, was that every other inmate was at least three years older than my thirteen years. I was later to find out that this was because it was thought that if I had been put with children of my own age, I would have been too violent and disruptive. Perhaps this is why I received special attention and came to be known as 'staff's pet'. Surprisingly, none of the other lads seemed jealous of my status and I never got any hassle because of it.

After living in Stanley House, most places would have seemed like hotels, but the three years I spent in the approved school were positively enjoyable and passed very quickly. I could now grow my hair to a reasonable length, wear long trousers and fashionable clothes and even enjoy the odd fag. In the children's home, it felt like I was being punished even when I hadn't done anything wrong but, now I was a criminal, life seemed to be much better. It made no sense, but I wasn't complaining.

I was used to mixing with older lads from my school days and soon made plenty of friends. Some even became like surrogate brothers to me but there were also plenty of lads who were only too willing to test my fighting abilities and, in the first few months, I became something of a coward. After about a year, my confidence began to grow and I found I could not only compete with the other inmates, but actually beat most of them. I gained a reputation as a pint-sized hardman and my ego swelled at the thought of being able to take on convicted criminals, who were considerably older and larger than me.

Other than football and rugby, I had no hobbies apart from looking after what was called 'Pet's Corner'. This was a little shed which contained all manner of small animals, which had been provided for the interest and amusement of the inmates. However, none of the other lads seemed at all interested or amused by the miniature menagerie and it was basically my own private place. I loved the animals and would spend hours in the shed cleaning, feeding and playing with them and I put a lot of hard work into it. Sometimes, my efforts to keep everything neat and tidy bordered on the over zealous.

The rabbit's hutch used to get covered in droppings, so I would clean it out and then scrub the bottom with bleach and water. One day, I returned to find that the rabbit had turned from white to yellow. It seemed to be alright, but I was puzzled and took the rabbit to the pet shop to have it checked out. It became apparent that the bleach I had been using was industrial strength and, when the rabbit had rolled in the sawdust on the bottom of its cage, it had got covered in the stuff. This dyed its fur from a lovely snowy white, to a strange, dirty shade of yellow.

Another time, I decided to obtain a slightly larger animal for pet's corner and set out to catch a sheep in the nearby fields. Unfortunately, the sheep did not want to be captured and, as I tried to drag it back to the castle, it began to bleat and make a lot of fuss. I was quickly rumbled and the sheep was returned to its rightful owner. The staff at the home weren't cross and took time to explain why I couldn't have the sheep, as it belonged to someone else and the impracticalities of looking after it in a shed. I put the whole incident down to experience and focused on the smaller members of the animal kingdom from then on.

I was running pet's corner so well that eventually there were simply too many animals in the small shed. In particular, the mice had been breeding at an incredible rate and were gnawing through the wooden cages and getting into the kitchens. The cook, who had always been very sympathetic to me and gave me left-over scraps to feed the animals, told me that some of the mice would have to go. Instead of just killing them, I decided to give them a chance. I bought a little kitten and then went up to the cage and warned the mice. "Listen, if any of you fuckers escape now, you've had it, this cat's gonna waste you. It's nothing to do with me 'cos these people will get rid of you all and if you do get out, it's at your own peril, it's death."

I thought that this was fair enough but I was concerned that maybe the kitten was too young to know how to kill mice and perhaps it needed to have its killer- instinct honed a little. I took my least-favourite mouse out of the cage and dangled it in front of the cat. To my surprise, it leapt up and ripped the skin off the tiny thing and then began to chew on its flesh. I was horrified that such a cute, furry, young animal could be so instinctively vicious and felt

15

very guilty about the incident for a long time.

Eventually, the mouse population expanded so dramatically, that it was decided they all must go, for the sake of hygiene and I was warned to get rid of them, or else someone else would come and dispose of them. I was very upset by this ultimatum but the way I dealt with the mice still troubles me today. I put groups of four or five mice into small, coffin-shaped boxes, nailed lids onto them and buried them in the garden. I hadn't intended to be cruel, it was just my way of trying to resolve the situation. Approved school is not a natural environment for a child of thirteen. It makes you do strange things.

Outside the approved school, I had nobody and so there was no reason to run away. Besides, if I did, I might have my sentence extended. The other inmates gave me hassle about it and, ironically, my reluctance to try and escape was viewed with concern by the staff. They considered it unhealthy for a young lad to be content with being incarcerated. They dragged me in front of a psychologist to see what was wrong and I quickly decided that, to keep everyone happy, I should run away. I wasted no time and was gone within the same day. I didn't make any effort to stay free and, in under twenty hours, I was caught and returned to the castle.

My second bunk from Dobroyd was more of a necessity and resulted from some attempted sexual experimentation. I had been playing for the local football team and a young girl called Gina Horsefield, a supporter of the opposition, had taken a shine to me. We arranged to meet at the next ground I was playing at and, halfway through the game, I pretended to be injured, so I could slope off into the woods with her. The plan was working perfectly and we were in the woods, kissing and touching each other up, when I heard a booming voice,

"You boy, get into the school." I couldn't see anybody, so we carried on.

"Cook, I've told you once, get into the school." I looked up and saw the headmaster on a hill above us. Scared about what punishment I would receive and what would happen to Gina, I felt I had no choice but to run away again.

I ended up in Moss Side in Manchester, where I met up with another lad from the school, Delroy Brown who was from the area and was a bit of a street kid. To me, he was just a good mate and together we got up to all sorts of trouble: thieving, nicking cars and joyriding. We had a great adventure, until we got hungry and decided to go back. The punishment was severe but it was worth it for the fun we had.

Delroy was one of a group of black lads in the home with whom I was friendly. They were all from Manchester and dressed in the latest fashions. I copied their clothes and became known around Dobroyd as a bit of a sharp dresser. I learned to dance like them and, at the school's annual dance, I got a chance to show off my skills. They were all impressed and this helped me to become accepted by them.

Some of the female staff had noticed the pride I took in my appearance and would bring in clothes for me. I would also steal clothes from the other inmates and store them in my grandmother's house when I went to visit. In my mohair suits, with wide vents, designed and made in Manchester, I was probably one of the most fashionable people in Doncaster and it made me feel pretty tasty.

During my time at Dobroyd, I found out that my mother had been readmitted to a mental hospital in Middlewood, Sheffield. I wanted to go and see her, so I disappeared again and made my way down to Sheffield, sleeping rough on the way. At the hospital reception, I found it remarkably easy to gain admission to the secure mental facility, and proceeded through countless corridors and wards before eventually finding it. I noticed there were locks on all the doors. It was very easy to identify my mother, as all the other patients were over sixty and she was only in her early thirties. Many of them appeared very disturbed and institutionalised and I didn't think my mum should have been on the same ward as them.

She had once been a very beautiful woman but now she looked rough and weary. She was smoking incessantly and her fingers were stained brown with nicotine. Worst of all, her hair had been hacked into the untidy basin cut which all mental patients were given at the time.

"Mum, it's Frank, your son." She stared blankly at me. There was no recognition. After three minutes, I mustered the courage to hold her hand and she turned slowly towards me and smiled but the smile seemed to pass straight through me. A male porter sauntered over with a smirk on his face.

"You won't get her to say anything," he sneered. Young as I was, I felt it was highly inappropriate for a such a man to be dealing with a vulnerable young woman like my mother, who could so easily have been taken advantage of. I explained that I was her son but he just shrugged indifferently and said it was time to go.

"I have to leave now, Mum," I told her and she grinned inanely at me. The whole experience had really disturbed me and I wandered in a daze through the endless, featureless corridors of the hospital. I finally found myself back in reception area, where I wasn't surprised to be met by a policeman. Apparently, the school had alerted the hospital that I might end up there, trying to find my mother. He escorted me back to Dobroyd, where the staff were sympathetic and did not give me a beating, the usual punishment for absconding.

After this affair, I was forced to see a psychiatrist once a month. I decided to steal the documents he compiled, regarding my case. I was still illiterate, so I gave them to my dorm-mate to read. They referred to my above average intelligence, which was tempered with emotional disturbance, hypomania and lack of self-confidence. The bottom line of the report contained this stark prophecy:

'Hope for this young man's future, is extremely bleak'.

Just after my sixteenth birthday, my three years were up and I was told I was free to leave. I got my release papers and then walked around the castle, having one last look and saying my goodbyes. I took so long that the staff said I could stay for dinner. By tea-time I was still there. The headmaster came over and said,

"Cook, are you still here?"

"Yes sir," I said, stating the obvious.

"Young man, you've got to go. Mr. Clayton, take him to the station because if you don't, he won't go." In fairness, I think he was right. If I hadn't been made to, I probably wouldn't have left but, as it was, I returned to my grandmother's in Doncaster and that is where the real problems began to happen.

Young Offender

Older, bigger, more street-wise and dressed to kill, I was back in Doncaster, living with my grandmother on the Balby Council Estate. I got a job as a welder and became quite handy but couldn't progress with the technical side, as I still couldn't read or write. I drifted out of employment and into petty crime, stealing from shops, nicking cars and doing burglaries.

The Northern soul scene was at its height in 1969 and I would often visit various clubs like the Wigan Casino, where I could show off my dancing. I would travel there with a little bag containing my aftershave, some Pernod and my drugs, usually Purple Hearts or speed. I really felt a sense of belonging to this little scene and it was like being part of a big family. In Doncaster, I would go to the local youth clubs and, fuelled by amphetamines and Pernod, frequently cause havoc. Twelve weeks after leaving approved school, I was banned from every youth club in Doncaster, for fighting and vandalism.

Although I loved my new, exciting lifestyle, my grandmother was double pissed off by my behaviour and felt I used her home like a doss-house, coming and going when it pleased me. I did respect her and didn't want to hurt her, but she annoyed me and I would often act very aggressively, sometimes screaming in her face and intimidating her. I was selfish and arrogant and her moaning never stopped me from getting up to whatever I wanted.

Jane, was a local girl and the daughter of a policeman and when she got mixed up with a young tearaway like me, the community was outraged. I lost my virginity to Jane but, unfortunately, she became pregnant, much to the horror of her father. Not fully understanding the seriousness of the situation, I was more worried about what her father would do to me, than the welfare of Jane and the unborn child. In the end, Jane got an abortion and I got a broken nose. Her family were so embarrassed by the whole incident, that they moved to Scotland and I quickly forgot about it and carried on with my criminal career.

My speciality was breaking into shops through the roof. I became so proficient at this, that there was an article in the local newspaper bearing the headline, 'Doncaster's Rooftop Invader'. This boosted my ego to the point where I would make deliberate mistakes during these burglaries, so that the police would know who I was. The Doncaster constabulary had never had to deal with things like this before and it took them months before they could pin anything on me. I used the money I made from the robberies to buy speed and alcohol. If I was a bit skint, I would drink cider instead of Pernod. I was either drunk or high all the time, which aggravated my increasingly callous and violent disposition.

Instead of trying to deal with my emotional problems, I went on a social suicide mission, destroying everything in my path. In some ways, I think I was subconsciously trying to get back into an institution, where my life would at least have some direction. If I was inside, I could also escape from Jane's dad who kept threatening to bash me, or set me up, using his police connections. Eventually, I was committing so many crimes, that it was only a matter of time before I got caught. Aged seventeen, I was hauled before the Quarter Session Court, where I pleaded guilty to a huge list of offences and was given six months in a detention centre. As the police took me down to the cells under the court, I reflected on my sentence. I knew it was going to be hard but then so was I and I would take everything they threw at me and come out the other side.

The police van bumped down the country lane, jostling me and the other detainee, a young Asian lad, called Peter Godfrey. They were taking us to a senior detention centre at Whetton in Nottinghamshire because the one serving our catchment area was full. It seemed that, once again, I would be thrown in with lads a lot older than myself but I didn't care; fighting them would make me tougher and equip me to deal with the world of hard men later on. As we arrived, one of the officers gave me a fag and said,

"Enjoy that, because it's the last one you're gonna smoke in a long time. After you get out of this van, you start saying 'sir'."

Saying 'sir' would pose no problems. I had been in institutions all my life and I knew that for self-survival, it paid to be deferential. Peter was new to the whole regime and held his head up high, nonchalantly acknowledging the officer's commands. His resistance was not to last long.

"Oi, you, Paki! You're in detention now," screamed one of the screws and whacked him round the ear. Another grabbed him by the collar and threw him to the ground. The other screws closed in and began laying into the poor bastard, who was only a fragile lad. At the same time, they shouted obscenities and racist names at him. His family, at the time one of the few ethnic minority families in the Doncaster area, had suffered a lot of racial abuse but it was nothing compared to what Peter was about to experience in detention. We all got good kickings by the staff on a regular basis, but Peter was subjected to more beatings and a constant torrent of abuse from them.

Peter was probably thinking that this was a tough way to start detention but, in fact, the reception ritual had barely started. We were bundled from one room to another, all the time being told what little scumbags we were and how we were going to be sorted out. In one room I was told to look at a poster of the Firearms Act on the wall. A screw told me to look at it more closely so I leaned nearer the wall.

"Even closer," he ordered, so I pushed my face an inch away from the wall. I'd gone totally boz-eyed and couldn't read a thing but pretended to, all the same. Suddenly, he punched the back of my head, smashing it against the wall and busting my nose. Blood was pouring everywhere and he just looked at me and laughed.

Next, it was bath time and we were told to strip off and stand on a line facing the bath, which had six inches of freezing water in it. Naked and shivering, we felt completely humiliated and were totally at the mercy of the guards. One of them walked in and, with a practiced manoeuvre, swept away our legs and pushed us into the bath. As Peter fell back, he cracked his head on the metal tap. Blood was spilling out from the gaping wound in his head, making the water a washed-out crimson.

"I'm fucking bleeding, let me get out," he cried, but the guards were not in slightest bit interested.

"Get washed in thirty seconds, or else, you horrible little bastards!" one of them screamed. We hastily cleaned ourselves and jumped out of the bath. Peter's white towel was bright red when he had finished drying himself and later, he had to have nine stitches in his head.

"When you open this door, your life becomes a misery," a guard warned us and by now I was ready to believe what he said. We picked up the mountain of regulation clothing with which we had been issued and walked out of the door, into a long corridor.

"See that fire extinguisher down there?" barked one of the guards. "Run to it and don't stop until you get there." Without hesitation, we both sprinted down the corridor with a gang of screws in hot pursuit, kicking, spitting and trying to trip us up. I stopped as I got to the first fire extinguisher but Peter kept on going. When I realised that the guards had no intention of stopping, I chased after him. We stumbled along, falling over, dropping bits of clothing and taking a fair few blows from the guards. Needless to say, I was relieved when they eventually locked us up in the induction unit for the night.

Before they left us alone, the guards told us to prepare our kit for an inspection in the morning. We didn't have a clue as to what kit they meant, how we should get it ready or where and at what time. The whole night was spent fretting about this and we both expected plenty more beatings the next day.

We remained on the induction unit for the first month of our stay in borstal, along with ten other lads. The brutality continued and we came to expect attacks by the guards at least once a day. When we were finally allowed into the mainstream, it was a great relief, as now we were just twelve lads among hundreds and statistically, the chances of being attacked were far less than when we were the sole focus of the guards' attention. The beatings weren't pleasant but, after the way my dad had treated me, they didn't bother me that much and they certainly didn't have the same emotional impact.

For some, the routine was just too harsh and I remember quite a few lads who flipped in detention centre. One person who springs to mind was a little Italian lad from Rotherham called Folleghani. We were out on parade, in the yard and one of the guards was reading out the names:

"Brown, Cook, Davis, Folleghani, Jamieson.... FOLLEGHANI! Who the fuck is Folleghani?"

"Me, sir," came the reply. The feeble voice matched by an even weedier physique.

"Come out here. Folle-fucking-ghani, where did you get a name like that?" shouted the guard.

"Me mam and dad, sir," replied the young lad, innocently. The guard was not impressed.

"What are you? A Russian, a Russian fucking spy?"

"No sir, an Italian."

"Italian! You coward." With that, the screw started slapping him viciously round the head, until he got back into line.

The next day, before the parade had even started, Folleghani teararsed off across the yard, screeching and waving his arms about. He had become so scared about what might happen to him that he had gone crazy and was making a run for the fence. It was a good four hundred metres to the fence and, when he got there, the screws were not far behind. He was halfway up the fence when they pulled him down. He disappeared in a throng of guards, all kicking and punching him and this was the last that any of us saw of Folleghani.

Every morning we had to shave, regardless of whether we needed to or not. Many of the lads hadn't even started to grow whiskers but were still forced to shave their skin. What made it worse, was that the razors were not always changed and you could end up using one that had been used by various other inmates over the week. This was not only unhygienic, but also meant that you might get a blunt razor, which would wreck your skin. The washroom was the place where inmates would make attempts on their lives, trying to slash their throats or wrists with the razors. I saw this happen on a number of occasions, but thankfully, none of them was fatal.

Some of the inmates used more devious methods to get out of detention. I got involved in one such scam and it reveals the very nasty, callous streak I had now developed. A lad called Pinney from Bury had decided that he wanted out and, as the only way to do this was through injury, he decided that he wanted his legs breaking. He was quite a strong, rough lad and I had had a few run-ins with him in the past but he came up to me and said he wanted me to break his legs. I was more than happy to do this but concealed my excitement and asked him if he was sure. He was dead set on getting out so we went to the gym where I propped his leg up on a bench.

Now, whether he wanted me to or not, I was going to break his legs. I selected a heavy, iron weights bar and lifted it up above my head. I brought it crashing down onto his leg but to my surprise it didn't break and the bar bounced off. He writhed on the floor in agony, clutching his shin, which had a huge dent in it and was already horribly discoloured.

"Again, again," he groaned, through gritted teeth. I couldn't believe he really wanted to be hit again but I obligingly stood back for another attempt. I raised the bar high above my head, and prepared to deliver the hardest whack I could. The bar flew down against his bare leg with such force it made me wince. I felt the vibrations pass through the bar but, incredibly, his leg had still not broken.

He writhed on the floor, in absolute agony, his leg in a terrible state and I decided enough was enough. The staff ran in to see what all the commotion was about and, when they saw his leg, they were very suspicious, as they knew we were not the best of friends. I told them he had fallen off the bench and although it was only a foot high, he backed up my story and nothing more was said. He was bandaged up and put straight back into his cell.

Like all the other lads, I hated the way we were treated in detention centre but I didn't let it get me down. I was becoming fit and muscular due to the training and I ate every last bit of the food that we were given. Inside me, hate was building up. I lay back and thought about when I would be let out. People would be made to pay for the way I had been treated.

It was early 1970 and I was out of detention centre and back with my grandmother in Balby. Ronnie was there too but Vinnie had followed in my footsteps and was in approved school. Nobody went to visit him, just like they had never visited me but I suppose it seemed normal for our family to be fractured. Sometimes, I even forgot I had another brother.

The mental hospital had decided that my mother was now well enough to leave and live on her own in a council tower block, near the town centre. She thought it was very posh but all the furniture was secondhand and the tower block was a bit of a dump. The hospital said she was better but she still had to go for injections for her schizophrenia, paranoia and hallucinations. All day she would sit around, drinking sherry, smoking fags and mumbling shit.

I suppose I should have felt sorry for her and tried to help her but I felt she still blamed me for tying her to my dad and I thought that the symptoms of her mental illness were her way of getting back at me. At first, I would try and figure out what her demented ramblings meant but when I couldn't understand, I became aggressive and began to despise her. I would threaten her to stop her talking crazily and I just couldn't understand that she wasn't responsible for the way she was. I even took knives to her in an attempt to get some normality out of her.

When Vinnie returned from approved school, I realised the extent of my mother's resentment towards me and finally came to accept that she was simply insane. Now, in Vinnie, I had a new partner in crime and the Cook brothers went into business. We would steal constantly, with me taking the lion's share of the profits. Every shop in the area was victim to our thieving and vandalism and we convinced ourselves that nobody knew that we were the perpetrators, when really it wa glaringly obvious.

I was also building up my own little firm who would break into the fashion shops in town and steal all the latest gear. Breaking into shoe shops was one of our favourite occupations but many of them only had the right shoes on display. One lad, Gilbert, would wear the odd shoes, even though he looked like a total prick. Even his mum would tell him to take them off but he had stolen them and was going to wear them. We looked pretty good in the expensive gear, which everyone knew was stolen, because we had no money.

Some of the rougher local girls were impressed by our flashy clothes and they would come down to the estates where we lived. They came from the same backgrounds as us and most of their dads were gypsies, rag and bone men or just thieves. Just like us, they were cheeky and rude and would match us in drinking, smoking and foul language but they were attractive enough to get us chasing them and they often caused us to fight amongst ourselves. We would call them sluts and slags but they would throw bricks at us and give as good as they got.

Our flat, on the seventh floor of Sanbeck House, was well known as a black spot in a bunch of tower blocks, mostly inhabited by decent, hardworking people. We played Motown, Reggae and Ska records at full volume on our secondhand record player, disturbing all the neighbours who would bang on the walls and swear at us. We couldn't care less and told them where to go or spat and threw bricks at them. An old couple downstairs would even ask us nicely to turn it down but their requests would always be met with, "Fuck off."

Another way we passed the time, was placing detonators in the car park under our balcony and throwing bricks onto them. The bricks usually missed and would hit people's cars, or passers by. If we actually hit a detonator, there would be a massive explosion which everyone in the flats would hear.

One day, the police came round and me and Vinnie decided to shoot them with an airgun. I took aim, fired but missed, so I passed the gun to Vinnie. He was aiming at the policeman but I told him to aim for the panda car instead. The pellet ricocheted off the roof of the car and flew straight into the copper's face, catching him just under the eye. Although nobody could prove it was us, everyone knew that the Cooks were responsible and there was outrage in the community for a while.

About this time, the council decided to build a network of subways around where we lived. We realised the potential for robbery in these places and I suppose we were the original muggers. At first, people's wallets seemed like easy pickings but on one occasion, I was given a good bashing by someone I tried to rob. Only slightly deterred, I decided that I would cajole Vinnie into doing the robbing for me. I concocted a plan, whereby we would wait in public toilets, until someone came in for a shit. Vinnie would hide in one of the cubicles and when the person sat down and dropped his pants, he would climb over the partition, bash him and make off with his wallet.

We waited by the toilets, until a suitable victim went in and Vinnie sneaked into the next cubicle. When he heard the unsuspecting man drop his trousers, he clambered over the partition with catlike ease and dropped down on him. I was outside, ready to receive the wallet and run in the other direction. There was a lot of banging and shouting coming from the cubicle and then Vinnie came flying out, battered all over and looking shit-scared. He slipped on the piss which was all over the floor and went crashing into the urinals. We hadn't bargained on the victim putting up any resistance and sprinted away as fast as we could. Vinnie was furious with me for getting him involved but I tried to placate him by saying he'd been unlucky and suggested trying the same plan, on the other side of town. Needless to say, he was far from keen on the idea.

My criminal activities were simply a means of getting money and what I was really bothered about was fighting and my macho image. I truly wanted to be the hardest man in the whole of Doncaster and went to great lengths to try and prove it. Every night I would go into town to drink and fight and I quickly became known as a nasty little pain in the arse.

Such a violent lifestyle soon resulted in my getting involved with all sorts of thugs and I started going to football matches with a big gang called the Balby Belvedere Boot Boys. Our leader was a kid called Richie Richardson, who was not a hard lad but he had charisma and we all loved him. He lived on Belvedere Road, Balby, hence the name of the gang and we were known as one of the hardest firms in the country. We fought with the fans of every visiting team and gave them all a good kicking; the only fans who ever beat us were the Millwall mob. Apart from Doncaster, we all supported Liverpool, because Bill Shankly was the greatest manager ever and Kevin Keegan was born in Balby and went to our school. We watched them whenever they played near Doncaster and had all the programmes and memorabilia.

Apart from being football hooligans, we were all thieves and I was now robbing cars, as well as shops. This was also when I committed my first armed robberies, although the people I was working with were not as enthusiastic, or as capable as me. I had no fear and was quite prepared to use a firearm but my accomplices were not dedicated criminals and were just attracted by the money. These preliminary attempts were usually bungled, or unsuccessful, but they gave me a glimpse of where my future lay. Unfortunately, these failed attempts at serious crime, along with the other offences I was committing, led to me receiving a six month to two year sentence in Borstal.

I loved Borstal because it was one of the few times in my life when I had no worries and was totally happy. It was as if a great burden had been lifted from my shoulders and I was finally in an environment tailor-made for people like me. The discipline, the hatred between staff and inmates, the violence I loved every minute of it. I can safely say that Borstal was where Frank Cook, the dangerous criminal, was born.

Whilst there, I made a very conscious decision to be a gangster and I wanted to be the best. Previously, I had no interest in learning to read but now I taught myself, so I could read every book about crime that I could get my hands on. There were plenty of people in there who could have taught me a thing or two about crime but I treated them with disdain. They were just small-time idiots in my eyes and I thought I was the fucking business.

The regime was just like detention centre, though perhaps not as hard and I thrived in the macho environment. My body was getting stronger and stronger and I was filling my mind with thoughts of the crimes I was going to commit on release. In the past, my criminality had merely been the result of my wayward upbringing and a need for cash. Now I was to become a professional criminal and there would be rules about which crimes I would commit and how I would do it. My past crimes seemed rather pathetic compared to what I was planning and, frankly, I was embarrassed by them. I gave up drink and drugs in favour of health foods and exercise and completely dedicated myself to a life of crime.

They let me out after one year and two months and, just before I went, an officer came up to me,

"They made a mistake sending you to Borstal Cook, you should have gone straight to prison. I'll see you in Wakefield nick".

On the train back to Doncaster, I thought about how I would start to put my plans into action and decided that there was no point in wasting any time. Within twenty minutes of getting off the train, I had committed a very serious armed robbery and made off through the alleyways, with a till full of dough. I went into a fashion shop and bought myself the best suit and shirt in the place. With the rest of the money, I bought an old banger. Now I was mobile, everything was in place.

In the next week, at the tender age of nineteen, I established myself as one of Doncaster's nastiest villains in a spree of violence which demonstrated my intent to the whole criminal fraternity. The top doormen in Doncaster were my main target and I went systematically, from club to club, showing them I meant business. I would swagger straight into a club, pretending not to even notice their presence.

"Hey kid, where are you going?" would be the usual response, upon which, I would turn round and bash them to the floor.

"I'm no kid, I'm Frank Cook," I would tell them. Sometimes, I would pull out two knives and offer one to the person I wanted to fight.

"I'm prepared to die," I would say, " but I'm not going to die because I'm going to win, I'm going to beat you."

Very soon, I had beaten nearly everybody and Doncaster's criminals realised that the only way to get rid of Frank Cook was to kill him. Even if I got beaten, I would come back with a lump of wood or an iron bar and make sure I really injured the person. I took over the jobs of the doormen I beat and this gave me prestige and a host of new criminal connections.

Doncaster is only a small town but in the seventies it was notorious for its vicious racketeering and gang rivalry. The two main gangs were the Shenton Firm and the Firm. My cousin Malcolm, an ex-boxer, was the leader of the Firm and so I quickly became involved in their activities. Image was all important and we would spend hours in the gym and on sunbeds, perfecting our macho posturing. I would train more than most, running thirteen miles every day, doing weights and constantly eating. I was perfect as Malcolm's right-hand man and personal Rottweiler. The Firm was mostly concerned with power and influence but I still saw myself as a professional villain, so I also committed crimes that were nothing to do with its activities.

Armed robbery was the crime that most attracted me, initially for the money but eventually, simply for the buzz. As I was using guns, I realised that the time might come when I had to shoot somebody. I knew I could cope with the thought of taking someone's life but I needed to know whether I could stand the sight of someone dying after I had shot him. To conduct my experiment on a human would have been a little extreme, so I drove out into the countryside and found a remote cow field. I took my shotgun, walked up to a cow and literally blew its head off. I stood over its body, staring into the mess of bone and gore that had been its head and felt a rush of excitement pass over me. I imagined a person lying in front of me and my feelings did not change. Mentally and physically, I now had all the makings of a very violent and dangerous criminal. I often cry now when I look back at such incidents and realise what they say about me as a person. I have to live with the shame but just try and get on with things.

My overwhelming desire to commit crimes was underscored by a dark and morbid fantasy that could have culminated in me spending the rest of my life in prison. The way I had been treated in the institutions I had lived in since I was eight had fostered a deep resentment within me of people in authority and, particularly, of those in uniform, which was rapidly turning into a pathological hatred. Even bus conductors would fill me full of venom and it took a great effort to control my feelings and stop them from spilling out into violence. One night, I lay awake, unable to sleep because of the rage curdling inside me. As I tossed and turned, it occurred to me that the only way to release the pent-up energy inside me was to kill a policeman.

With my brain in overdrive, I jumped out of bed and pulled on a tracksuit and a dark hat. I left the house with my gun and walked down the dual carriageway that led from Balby into the town centre, watching out for police cars. When I reached some shops, I stopped and began to tamper with a cigarette machine, trying to look suspicious and arouse attention. I hoped and prayed that a police car would notice me and come over. My only precondition was that the policeman had to touch me, then I would blow him away. All he had to do was manhandle me and I would execute him without hesitation.

Eventually, a car did come over and I could barely contain the excitement rising within me.

"What are you doing there?" asked the policeman in the passenger seat.

"Nothing," I mumbled, as suspiciously as possible. He looked at me and then turned to the driver, muttered something and they drove off. It hadn't worked this time but my passion had not subsided, so I came back every day for the next week or so, desperate for one of them to touch me and, in my eyes, justify my killing them. Unbelievably, not one policeman got out of his car and I still can't believe how lucky I was that they didn't. My desire cooled a little and I ceased my nightly walks but I kept my gun with me all the time and was ready to use it, the moment anyone crossed me.

Armed robberies were becoming an obsession and I went on a binge of twelve in quick succession before finally being caught during the thirteenth. Some were pretty dismal failures but that was mostly because the people I was working with were not as daring or dedicated as I was. I made mistakes as well and, during one job on a building society in the city centre, I put my balaclava on wrongly and ended up breathing through one eye hole and looking through the nose hole. I couldn't see what I was doing properly and, as I ran into the foyer, I tripped over a coffee table and went sprawling to the floor. We didn't get any money and were lucky to get away without being caught.

The last robbery failed when my driver bottled it when the alarm sounded and sped off. I was left to try and escape across town, being chased by security guards, policemen and various members of the public. I made it to the other side of the city centre before ending up under a heap of people, all baying for my blood.

"Ah, it's our Frankie!" the officers exclaimed, when they pulled off my mask. They were delighted to have finally caught the vicious thug who had been terrorising the town. I had brought a whole new level of criminality to the streets of Doncaster and it shocked and disturbed a lot of people, from both sides of the law, who breathed a sigh of relief when I was given a six year sentence for my numerous misdemeanours.

The First Sentence

I was sent to the notorious Armley prison in Leeds, a place which I later came to know as the 'Belly of the Beast'. My time in Borstal had established my reputation and prison would reinforce it but I was acutely aware that I was going to be away for a long time and there would be many people ready to slag me off and try to take my place. I felt I had to remain as hostile as possible, so that people on the outside would get to hear of me and know that Frank Cook would be coming back. I was just as dedicated to my life of crime as ever and, as I was fighting against the law, I now saw myself as a prisoner of war.

At every opportunity, I would cause trouble or try to escape. I saw the prison officers as enemies and did not communicate with them. Most of the other prisoners didn't act like me and I viewed them as pathetic morons, so I didn't speak to them either. This kind of behaviour soon got me a three week stint in solitary, followed by another, virtually straight away. As this came to an end, I was selected for a transfer to Lancaster prison from a group of thirty other prisoners.

When you first arrive at a prison, you are put on the reception wing before being allocated to a normal wing. For some reason, I never got off the reception wing at Lancaster and it began to annoy me. I became extremely disruptive and, with the help of others, planned several disturbances. Before anything happened, the prison authorities got wind of these plans and put me into isolation.

Unlike normal location, where you can talk to other inmates and exercise with them once a day, isolation means you are truly alone. You get no exercise and the only person you come into contact with is the guard who brings you your food. At first, I tried to be resilient, but the crushing effects of loneliness soon began to affect my psychological well-being. I became crazier and crazier and started to go wild and smash up my cell. I was ranting and raving so they gave me injections of a drug called Largactil, which was created by the Russians in the fifties to be used in the control mental and political patients. In America, it was used to slow down cattle, as it increased appetite, causing them to become obese. To the prisoners, it was simply known as the original liquid cosh. It was supposed to sedate me but I had so much energy that it didn't work and just made me more unstable.

I would dent the door by smashing a metal chair against it and, anything that was not tied down, I flung about. I was so mad, that I would throw my shit about or rub it up the walls and in my hair. To try and tranquillise me more effectively, they used a horse sedative called Peraldehyde, which was so potent that it had to be injected with a metal syringe, as it would melt a plastic one. It rendered me totally moronic and made my psychological condition even worse.

The screws were constantly trying to get statements out of me which would enable me to be released from isolation but I wouldn't allow them into my cell. The only man whom I allowed to come in was the prison vicar, Canon Hodgson. I respected the man as he didn't try to push his religion onto me, he was simply there to listen. He didn't mind that my cell was covered in shit, or that I looked and acted like a complete animal and he was very sympathetic to me towards me.

"Frank, why don't you just sign the statements so you can get out of here?" he would often ask me.

"No, because I live here and I'm going to die here," I would always tell him.

The drugs were making me hallucinate and I thought that there were ghosts in my cell, so I decided to ask the Canon whether he believed in ghosts. I was very worried that he would laugh at me but when I told him, he looked at me very seriously and said,

"Tell me what you have seen Francis." He listened intently to what I told him and said that he did believe in ghosts and that he had actually seen one. He even said that he thought it was likely, as it was where lots of Scottish people had died and he said their souls were not at rest. I couldn't believe that he didn't think I was nuts.

"Fucking hell, I've seen these ghosts you're talking about, Father,"

I exclaimed excitedly.

"Why don't you come out, away from the ghosts, Francis?" he replied, trying to coax me back into the mainstream prison.

"No, I'll do the ghosts in. I'll freak them out 'til they leave me alone," I told him and every time I saw one, I would scream at it, until it went away.

"See, even ghosts can't take me," I would say to myself.

I lingered in the isolation cell, my condition steadily worsening, until one day I was told that I had visitor. They wouldn't allow me to go into the normal visitors' room, so they put me in a special cell where I had to speak through glass. The drugs were making me see about six of everything but I made out my cousin Malcolm, behind the glass. He looked at me and said,

"How are you Frank?" and I could see the shock on his face as he saw the state I was in and the tears welling in his eyes,

" What are they doing to you?" I didn't answer and he repeated his question,

"What's happened to you? What are they doing to you, Frank?" I looked at him and grinned.

"They're trying to kill me," I said. At this point, sadness overwhelmed me and I began to cry as well. Malcolm looked at me pityingly,

"I can't stand this Frank, I've got to go."

"Oi, you!" he shouted to a prison officer. "Get over here you, you cunt and get me the governor."

Immediately, a door opened and an officer quickly escorted me back to my cell. I sat there slightly puzzled as to what had just happened. The cell door opened and I was taken into another room, full of people. There was a doctor there, the chief officer, two medical officers, the governor and loads of screws. The doctor spoke first.

"How long have you been in there?" I just grinned and said,

"You all know how long I've been in there, it's been over six months."

"You've been in there for six months, Cook? How much exercise do you get?" he asked me.

"I used to get one hour a day for the first eight weeks but none any more," I told him.

"You mean to say that you haven't seen another human being for four months?" he asked, in obvious disbelief.

"Not apart from these screws." He just laughed, incredulously. The high-ranking officers muttered amongst themselves.

"What medication is he being given?" demanded the doctor and, when he was told, he seemed very annoyed.

"You can't use that on him, it's far too strong." He insisted that I was weaned off it but by a gradual process, otherwise, he warned, I would be at risk of a heart attack. He also ordered that I was to be immediately removed from the isolation cell and transferred into hospital.

The doctor left and I was returned to the isolation cell to await transportation to a hospital. Later in the night, a screw came in with a cup of something and told me to drink it. I didn't resist but was so drugged that I spilled most of it down my face, which was covered with a scraggy beard. Whatever was in it sent me to sleep and, when I awoke, I was strapped to a stretcher, being carted through the prison corridors. I was put in the back of a van and off I went to Liverpool.

The van drove straight through the gates and round to the back of the prison, where the hospital wing was situated. The receiving doctor was Doctor Daz, who said he wouldn't sign the warrant sheet, as he refused to accept a patient prisoner. The officers escorting me had no other option than to drive up the M62 to Manchester, where they took me to Strangeways Gaol. I was accepted there and then pumped full of the same medicine and thrown into a padded strip cell.

Thankfully, one of the prison officers was a little old Irish lady, who was very compassionate and showed me a lot of kindness. She helped me to gradually wean myself off the medication and get back into mainstream prison. Obviously, it was better to be on normal location again but things were still hard. My reputation had preceded me, which meant problems from staff and inmates. I continued to be hostile to the staff and was constantly in trouble. The staff watched me twenty-three hours a day and, although I was slightly better, I was still very volatile and certainly not mentally balanced. I had regular visits to the psychiatrist, which were boring and repetitive and didn't help me in the slightest.

The last part of my sentence was served in Liverpool's Walton Prison, where my behaviour was exactly the same as in Manchester. It was here that I learned what prison was really like.

I was still a fitness fanatic and outside I had always eaten plenty of healthy food. I now found that the food was foul-tasting, unhealthy shit that was so bad that I actually feared for my life at first. Breakfast was always porridge, which doesn't sound too bad, until you taste it. Sometimes, we would get eggs, which were okay and bread which was always stale and wafer thin. We called the tea 'diesel' because you could see straight through it and it didn't taste much better than diesel either.

Lunchtime was even worse. There would usually be soup for starters, concocted from the leftovers of the previous day's meal and thickened with porridge. It had virtually no taste but the texture was so revolting it made you retch. Then there was always something involving spuds, usually a potato pie and some meat left over from the day before. There were always plenty of vegetables but they tasted rubbery and were so overcooked that there was no goodness in them. The sweet was either 'duff pudding', made from Yorkshire pudding mix with a few raisins in it or rice pudding made with watery milk. It was called the sweet, although it didn't taste sweet. There's nothing sweet in prison.

The final meal of the day was probably the worst: more spuds and some beans or spaghetti and some razor-thin corned beef. There was so little meat, that you literally couldn't taste it. You might also get a bit of bread with butter, which was actually coloured lard.

What most inmates did to cope with this nauseous diet, was to buy a huge bottle of brown or red sauce and smother every meal in it. This camouflaged the horrible taste and made it just about edible. Nearly every prison I have been in, offers virtually exactly this menu and it appals me that the Home Office can still get away with it.

The cooks were inmates and, although their pay was good, their hours were long, so they often slept in their kitchen whites. It was strange, but the kitchens always seemed to attract dirty, unhygienic men and there were never any checks on cleanliness. We all knew what they got up to and what they put in the food. A favourite trick was to put detergent in, to give everyone the shits.

One time, I got into the kitchen and was horrified by what I saw there. There were carcasses hanging up, with skulls and cross bones printed on the side. Underneath, it said 'not fit for human consumption'. The porridge oats were Grade One Canadian pig-meal, again marked unft for human consumption. There was some decent meat, but that was being saved by the cooks for themselves and for the officers' dinners. The kitchens were filthy and infested with mice and cockroaches.

In fact, the whole prison was infested with mice, as is nearly every prison in the country. The vermin population is kept in check by the cats, which are also a part of prison life. I have no idea how these animals manage to get into prisons, but no matter which one you go to, there are always a few resident cats. They were mangy, scruffy beasts but were always quite plump because of the abundance of food to scavenge. At night, they would keep you awake with their fighting and mewing. Prison birds were also a strange breed, always more ragged than normal birds and a depressing sight.

One of the things that most disturbed me initially, was the homosexuality in prison. At that age, I thought that homosexuality was very perverted and the last thing I expected hardened criminals to be doing was buggering each other. I'd seen it going on in the children's home but that seemed to be different, almost normal. These were robbers, tough guys, men who I looked up to and here they were getting up to all kind of perverted stuff.

Most of the hardmen used to slag off queers but I found that the ones who went on about it the most, were usually the ones who were up to it all the time. I was sickened. To me it was deviant, weird, not fucking on, basically, but soon I came to realise that, in prison, it is accepted as the norm.

It usually went on just before lock-up, sometimes in the showers but mostly in the cells. Some inmates were quite blatant, while others were more secretive and you only found out if you accidentally stumbled across them. Most men just did it purely for sexual gratification, the only way they could get a shag in the absence of women. Then there were the men who were gay before they came to prison. The third, more sinister group, were the perverted element, who used sex to enforce power. These were the rapists who would violate a man to destroy his dignity, just to exert power and control. Often, there were gang rapes and the only way to deter them was to show you were not weak or vulnerable. I was always left alone, as people accepted that, even if they gang raped me, I would come back and kill, or very seriously injure, every one of them but I felt sorry for the weaker inmates who were easy targets.

These things go on every day in prison and, at first, you are appalled but you learn to deal with them because you have to, if you want to get by. To survive, you have to learn to cope with the most terrible and disgusting things because if you don't, you crack up. Only afterwards, do you realise that you've destroyed your emotions in the process. This was what I found to be one of the most damaging things about prison and is the reason why many long-term inmates find it impossible to revert back to life on the outside.

Prison is such a strange place that normal behaviour seems out of place. If you thought about the horror of prison in normal terms, you would soon go mad. You have to try and suppress your feelings, so that what you experience eventually seems normal. The terrible irony of it is that, when you have denied your true emotions for so long, it is very hard to recover them and, when you leave the prison environment, you find yourself broken, a shell of what you used to be. The better you become at coping with prison, the worse you are at living a normal life.

When I was eventually released, the doctor gave me an envelope to give to my GP and I was let out onto the busy Walton Road. I had the option of getting the bus or a taxi. When I got to the bus stop, everybody was staring at me and I became very paranoid, so I jumped into the nearest taxi. My first destination was a denim shop called Flemings, which I had been told by a Liverpudlian made up great jeans for you. A week before, I had sent them my measurements and, when I got there, I found the jeans were a perfect fit. They were the only thing I had to wear on release and, back in Doncaster, they gave me something to be proud of and helped me get control of my paranoia.

On the train, on the way back, I was very uncomfortable. I felt it was going too fast and that all the passengers knew where I had been and what I had done. I felt soiled. As we approached Doncaster, mixed feelings of excitement and fear played through my mind and I became so confused that I had to go into a toilet and calm myself down. What I needed was a pint, so I ran across the road and into the nearest pub. Because of my fitness regime, I hadn't had any alcohol for quite a long time. The first pint definitely had the desired effect, so I had another and another after that. The pub was full of villains and, inevitably, I got talking to them all.

My self-consciousness and anxiety were still intense and I was constantly worrying about what they had all been up to in my absence and whether they thought prison had broken me. During a difficult conversation, I realised that it was going to be very difficult to re-establish myself in the Doncaster criminal underworld but my appetite for crime had not abated and I was determined to succeed.

Before I could even think about getting my career back on track, I had to think about where I would live. I hadn't had any contact with my mum since I went to jail but I turned up at the tower block, as I had nowhere else to go.

A very frail and ugly-looking woman answered the door, whom I could hardly recognise as my mother. Her condition had been deteriorating when I left, but now she looked awful and I wondered what was wrong with her.

"Hi, mam," I greeted her, smiling.

"Ooh! hello, Frank," she said, flinging her arms around me and giving me a kiss. It was as if I was the prodigal son returning. I hugged her back and walked into the living room. She offered me a fag but I said no, so she offered me some of the sherry she was drinking. I accepted, as I felt that alcohol was helping me to stay calm. We got talking and eventually she asked me where I was planning on living.

"I want to live here, mam," I told her, expecting her to say yes, after the welcome she had given me.

"I don't want you to live here, Frank, all you do is cause trouble."

"But mam, I've got nowhere else to go, I've got to stay here."

"Well, if you stay, you're going to have to pay rent and you'd better behave." I was in no position to argue, so I accepted her offer and started to settle in.

Gang Warfare

I was now ready to start thinking about resuming my criminal career and so I paid a visit to my cousin Malcolm and re-established myself as a member of The Firm. The Firm posed as nightclub bouncers and walked round in black suits and bow ties but, beneath the thin veneer of respectability, its members were all ruthless criminals, involved in armed robbery and various other types of serious theft. I asked Malcolm to get me a job on the door of a particularly rough club in the city centre, called Zhivago's, and he duly obliged.

Life in the Firm was good. Our days were spent in the gym or on the sunbeds, building up the image that was so important in maintaining the gang's status. Sometimes we would go jogging, or engage in marathon fighting bouts. Best of all were the women, who were literally queuing up to shag us. I couldn't get enough and fucked all manner of females at every available opportunity. Exercise, violence and sex became like drugs to me and I would actually suffer if I was deprived of any of them.

Because of my family connection to Malcolm, I immediately assumed the role of second-in-command. Malcolm, because of power and pressure, felt vulnerable and distrustful of the other gang members and we both constantly reassured each other that our status was impregnable. It was ironic that the stress of maintaining the appearance of hard and uncaring villains made us very sensitive to each other's feelings. The other members of the gang recognised how close me and Malcolm were and this gave me a psychological hold over them. The set up was good and I was content to loyally follow Malcolm, knowing that if he was removed, I was ready to step into his place.

My paranoia was still a problem and I imagined that I had a lot of grievances that simply did not exist. This resulted in me being excessively hostile to a lot of people, generally reinforcing their perception of me as a dangerous nutter. At the time, I had no idea that my behaviour instilled such fear in others and, when people acted strangely because they were intimidated by me, I thought they had a problem with me. This fuelled my distrust and made me even more aggressive. I was the only real gunman in the Firm and I later found out that even the other members were scared of me.

I was still living in the high-rise flat and my mum seemed quite happy with the whole arrangement. I would buy her daily bottle of sherry instead of rent and I didn't cause her any problems, as I was usually out with the Firm, or working on the door at Zhivago's. Her health was always poor but, one day, she seemed particularly ill, so I reluctantly called out the doctor. I didn't really care about her, so it was a total pain in the arse having to wait around, while he carried out his little tests. When he had finished, he called me to one side and said,

"You do know your mother has cancer, don't you?" I had no idea but it certainly explained why she seemed so decrepit. The news came as a surprise but it didn't really bother me.

"How long does she have to live?" I asked him, matter-of-factly.

"I can't say exactly but it could be only a matter of months, or even weeks." I had no feelings of love towards her but I wanted to make the little time she had left bearable, so I tried to be nice to her and continued to buy her sherry. My real priority though, was my rapid ascent to the top of the criminal sub-culture.

In five weeks, I had already re-established myself as one of Doncaster's top crooks and as a man not to be messed with. Being a member of the Firm meant people gave you respect and we would swagger round town as if we owned the place. Unfortunately, trouble was brewing and my new lifestyle was soon to come to an abrupt end.

The Firm did not have an unchallenged hold on all of the organised crime in the town and our direct rivals were a gang called the Shenton Firm. Whereas we used brain as well as brawn to carry out our criminal activities, the Shenton Firm was purely and simply a heavy mob. Their speciality was protection rackets and they used violence to extort money from bookies, publicans and market-stall holders. They were feared and hated throughout the community and by many villains. I was vaguely aware that they were supposed to be our rivals, but I was on speaking terms with most of them and just saw them as people from the same mould as myself. It came as a big surprise when the rivalry suddenly erupted into an orgy of violence.

It all started in Zhivago's, on a night when I was working on the door and Shenton and his boys came in. Apparently, the assistant manager of the club,

Alan Bailey, who was also a member of our gang, had been giving them money to pay for protection. Tonight, they were coming to get more cash from him but, at the last minute, he changed his mind and a fight broke out between him and one of Shenton's heavies, Patrick Ronan. I joined in and we battered Ronan and threw him out of the club.

"The Firm are going to be right into you," were his parting words and, from then on, I knew things were going to get nasty.

Over the next eighteen hours, five people were seriously injured and countless others were both physically and psychologically wounded by the violent repercussions of the scuffle in the club. Doncaster, a small town, not used to such goings on, was the scene of gang warfare, that was likened to that in Chicago in the 1920s.

Early on the morning of the twenty-third of September, Ronan caught up with Bailey, at the Woolpack pub, in the market in Doncaster. Along with Shenton and two other members of the gang, they gave Bailey a right good kicking and slashed his back. They also warned him that I would be next. Unwillingly, I had been drawn into this conflict and, although the prospect of another spell inside was far from appealing, I knew I would have to act. I went down to the banks of the River Don and dug up one of the many guns I had buried there, got hold of some cartridges and returned home to think about some sort of plan.

I wanted to get revenge on Shenton's lot but without risking getting myself killed. The scheme I came up with seemed foolproof at the time but, as with all my devious schemes, it didn't quite work out according to plan. I wanted to wound one of Shenton's firm badly enough for him to get the message but not in a way that would seriously damage him and get me sent down. Next, I was going to make an anonymous phonecall to the police, telling them what I had done. I was going to pretend that I had a hit list of all the rest of Shenton's Firm, so that the police would go and give them protection. With the police keeping an eye on them, they wouldn't be able to come after me and, hopefully, the conflict would come to a relatively peaceful conclusion. Unfortunately, this was nothing like the way things actually turned out.

My target was a man called Davis and I drove to his house, crept round the back and peered through the bedroom window. I couldn't believe what I saw – Davis and his latest woman, passionately shagging for all they were worth. I was a pretty cruel person but even I wouldn't have shot a man in the back at such a vulnerable moment. Instead, I ran round to the front of the house and shouted to him through the letter box and then dashed back to the bedroom window.

Inside, he was hastily pulling up his trousers, while his none-too-lovely woman draped herself in unbecoming wraps. I lowered the gun to the crack in the curtains and prepared to let rip. Suddenly, a terrifying thought hit me. What if the glass flew back into my face when I let the gun off? I now realise it wouldn't have happened but, in that split second, my mind wasn't functioning rationally. I turned away and fired in what I thought was the right direction. The sound of the gun going off and glass smashing, filled the air. I turned round to assess the damage I had done to Davis and realised I had missed him and peppered his bird's shoulder instead. I sprinted back up the passageway, annoyed that I had not managed to bring my attack to a successful conclusion.

The complete fuck up that had just occurred was such a feeble attempt at resolving the power struggle that I decided to go into town and search out other members of Shenton's gang. I entered the pool room that was their favourite haunt and was surprised not to find any of them in there. I hung around for a while but nobody showed, so I went back to Malcolm's, to review the situation and plan our next move.

When I got there, Malcolm told me that Shenton's gang had caught my brother Ronnie in town and given him one fucking good beating. A whole bunch of them had beaten him until he was unconscious and then thrown him through a glass window and left him in a pool of his own blood. Ronnie had nothing to do with our gang and was barely aware of the extent of my criminality. What was very frightening about the attack, was that nobody had helped Ronnie, even though it happened in the middle of town, in broad daylight, because they were so scared of Shenton's Firm.

Bailey called to tell us he had been released from hospital and didn't know what to do. My super-cool cousin just leaned back in his chair, gently puffing on his cigar and sent a taxi to fetch him. As we waited, he announced that another plan was needed and I agreed. What we decided to do, was to try and get Bailey to do our dirty work for us. When he got back, we tried to incense him, by reminding him how badly he had suffered at the hands of Shenton's Firm. With his wounds still smarting, our approach had the desired effect and very soon he was cursing and swearing and telling us what he'd like to do to them. When he was really raging, I offered him my gun and suggested he should go and take his revenge on them. I suppose it was a bit cruel, but this was a matter of survival and, after all, it was him who had caused all the trouble in the first place.

Bailey took the gun but wanted me to drive him into town. I agreed but said we should stop at my mother's flat, to gather our thoughts first. As we approached the flats, I loaded the shotgun and cocked the firepin, expecting trouble. The moment we arrived at the front door I knew something was wrong, as the hallway light was off and my mother was obsessed with always leaving it on. The door was closed but had been damaged, so we entered very cautiously.

The flat was completely destroyed, with furniture scattered everywhere and blood on the walls and floor. In the bedroom, blood was congealing on the white bed linen. Silently, I moved towards the lounge, not knowing what I would find in there. I tried to push the door but there was something behind it. I pushed harder and managed to get into the room, to be confronted by my mother's body, sprawled out in front of me. The instant I saw her, I knew she was dead. Bailey followed me in and couldn't believe what he saw. He knelt down beside her and started checking for signs of life.

"Call an ambulance Frank," he urged, in panic. Indifferently, I turned and walked out of the flat and went to look for a phonebox. My mother was dead and Shenton and his gang were definitely to blame. I knew that before the day had finished, I would take my revenge on them.

When I got back to the flat, Bailey was sitting by my mother, crying.

"What the fuck are you crying for?" I asked him.

"Look at your mum, Frank. Look at her, she's dead," he sobbed.

"This is out of hand, Frank," he went on, "your mum's dead and more people are going to get hurt tonight." At this point, I realised that Bailey would be no use to me at all. To him, the world of homicide was a distant fantasy and when he actually came to see a real corpse he fell apart. To me, the fact that people might die, was no big deal. In fact, in the circumstances, it seemed a very natural thing to happen. What did bother me, was the origin of the blood which was spattered all over the flat. It certainly wasn't my mother's, which meant something else terrible had happened here. There was no way to find out now, so I pushed it to the back of my mind.

The ambulance arrived and and the ambulancemen came into the flat.

"Which one of you is coming with her?" one of the drivers asked us.

"Neither of us," I replied, "we'll visit her in the hopital, if she comes round." As soon as they had left, my mind returned to the task in hand and, after I had calmed Bailey down, we drove into the town centre to look around. I decided that Bailey should attempt to lure all the members of Shenton's Firm into one pub, whereupon I would calmly walk in with my shotgun and execute them all.

The town centre looked as it always did, full of normal people going about their business but I could detect a sinister undercurrent, as we paced about the pavements and subways. As we entered one underpass, there was a sudden, loud rush of feet coming towards us. Bailey turned and looked hopefully towards me, as if he expected me to take them all on single-handedly. I swung round and started firing the shotgun indiscriminately in their general direction. I let off thirteen rounds of ammunition but, unbelievably, only one of Shenton's men was slightly injured. Two of the rounds went through a bus window, one went through a pub window and the town was thrown into a state of chaos.

People everywhere dived for cover, cars crashed and the sound of screaming filled the air. I was oblivious to everything around me and totally focused on the task in hand. Shenton's men scattered, so I set off in pursuit of one of them, whom I eventually managed to pin to the floor. I pointed my gun to his head, only to find that I had run out of ammunition and he was able to make his escape. Their gang were now scattered across the whole town centre and the field of battle had now increased in size dramatically.

During the course of the battle, Bailey and I had become separated, so I decided to seek him out, so we could decide on our next move. I found him licking his wounds down by the railway track and together we decided to go for a drink in a quiet pub. At this time, I was strictly teetotal but I felt a stiff drink might help me to think straight. After one pint, I started to feel a lot more relaxed, so I had a few more and, in no time, I was bragging to him about what I was going to do to Shenton and his firm. Bailey slipped off to use the phone, which made me suspicious, so I went over to see who he was calling. Bailey was supposed to be a gangster, but really he wasn't cut out for it and, when he heard what I was going to do, he had decided to call the police and tell them to come and arrest me. I literally had to grab him and physically drag him out of the pub.

Bailey was obviously shitting himself at the prospect of more violence and he pestered me to go and get rid of the gun. In the end, we went down to the banks of the River Don and I buried the gun there. The town centre was now swarming with police, some of them armed and some with dogs. We slipped up a sidestreet and into a nightclub, where I quickly took the manager and his associate hostage. Unfortunately, someone had seen me entering the building and the police had it surrounded in a matter of minutes. The area was sealed off and extra police were drafted in from Leeds, Sheffield and Wakefield.

I was using broken glass and bottles quite effectively to keep the manager and his associate hostage, but I didn't have any viable plans regarding my escape. The police were constantly calling the club and making me increasingly nervous. I tried making threats, saying I would kill the hostages and claiming I had a gun but, in the end, I knew I couldn't win and decided to give myself up. Stupidly, I felt an immense ego boost when I was told to come out with my hands up, but this feeling was short-lived, as I realised I was inevitably facing another lengthy prison sentence.

With alarming speed, I was handcuffed and rushed to Doncaster Police Station and put into an interview room. I told the police that I would take them to the spot where I had buried the gun, intending to shoot one of the officers and escape. When we got there, the officers wouldn't let me go near the site and, luckily, I didn't get the chance to carry out my plan.

The authorities were still worried about gang violence and they decided to keep me away from the five defendants from Shenton's Firm. They were housed in Leeds Prison, while I was taken to the infamous Risley Remand Centre to await trial.

Inside Again

I knew I was going down for a long time and, as I had only been out for a matter of weeks since serving the last sentence, I wasn't very happy, to say the least. Characteristically, I vented my anger by reverting to the violent and disruptive behaviour that had typified my last stint in prison and attempted to cause havoc at every opportunity.

When I got into my cell, I noticed it was dusty and could do with a bit of a clean, so I made a mental note to brush it the next day. The doors were opened and the brush was given to an IRA man called Duffy who didn't sweep his cell but just sat around chatting with a sex offender. I went into his cell and asked him if I could use it when he had finished and, in an offhand manner, he just said, "yeah", but didn't bring me the brush. This was repeated on the following two days and I was getting pretty pissed off, so I went into his cell and asked him if he had a problem about the brush. He turned round aggressively, holding the brush in his hands and with that, I snatched it from him and smashed it over his head. The handle snapped and I started jabbing him in the face with the splintered end. He fell to the floor screaming and clutching his injured face, upon which, I leapt on him and tried to strangle him. By this time, the screws had heard the commotion and ran in and pulled me off. They placed me on another part of the block but my rating was now changed to a 43B. The 43 meant I was a protected prisoner but the B was because I was regarded as a danger to both staff and inmates. I was also branded an 'E' man, which meant I was expected to attempt to escape.

Nothing much happened on the block and I was just waiting for the trial when, out of the blue, one of the officers came in and announced that the police were here, to talk about other crimes I had committed. This took me by surprise and, as I was escorted to the interview room, I tried to remember all the things I'd been involved in and how I could talk my way out of them. When I actually got there, I realised that the bastard screws had been lying and the visitor was really a prostitute I had met once before, called Pat.

There are many cases of men raping women but you rarely hear of the reverse scenario. My first encounter with Pat proved that it does occasionally happen. She was a very big girl and when a spot of petting got out of hand, she forced herself on me and demanded that I have sex with her. I made it very clear that I was not interested but she would not take no for an answer. I just had to lie there and pray that it ended soon. Anyway, it would be an understatement to say that I was surprised to see her again, particularly under these circumstances.

I sat down, confronting her face to face.

"Why have you come?" I asked her, genuinely puzzled.

"I've brought you some food and some money but the officers say I can't give you the money, so I'll send it to you," she replied.

"How did you get here?" I inquired, curious as to why a woman I had only met once, should travel all this way to see me.

"I hitched and I'm a bit wet but I'm okay," she said and I noticed she was actually soaking.

"Frank," she said, "I want to write to you while you're in prison." My heart went out to the girl. She had inexplicably made the effort to come and see me and she actually cared about what was going to happen to me but, at the same time, I knew I couldn't reciprocate her feelings. I was touched by what she had done but I knew she wanted more than I could ever promise her.

"Pat, I'm very grateful for the fruit but keep the money. I'm not the type of person who writes letters and I just want to do my time, on my own," I told her. I thought this might upset her and that she would get up and leave, but she was unperturbed.

"Frank, I don't mind if you don't write back, because I'm going to write anyway." I couldn't say anything to that, so I thanked her once more for the fruit and then she left.

Just as she had promised, letters soon started arriving and I found that they were actually quite interesting. They usually concerned current affairs in Doncaster and they helped me keep in touch with the outside world. In the end, contrary to what I had told her initially, I began to reply to her weekly letters.

Pat was able to clear up the mystery of whose blood was all over my mum's flat that day when we found her. It turned out to be my brother Ronnie's. On the day of the battle with Shenton's Firm, he had been innocently walking through the town centre, minding his own business, when he was spotted by some of Shenton's gang. Even though he wasn't involved with the Firm in any way, they beat him savagely and then flung him through a shop window, just because he was related to me.

Nobody came to his aid and, when he started to come round, he dragged himself to my mother's flat to call an ambulance. Naturally, once there, he thought he was safe but Shenton's gorillas decided to go back for some more and literally followed the trail of blood. They kicked the door in and battered Ronnie to within an inch of his life. They didn't notice my mum, who was hiding in another room but, in her weakened condition, just the trauma of hearing what was happening was enough to finish her off. This discovery enraged me and I felt immensely frustrated that I hadn't killed the lot of them when I had the chance.

My trial eventually came round after three months in Risley and I was transported to Sheffield Crown Court. The trial was held in Sheffield, as it was considered to be too volatile a case to be held in Doncaster and there were fears that there could be a repeat of the violence. Six of the largest policemen I had ever seen surrounded me at all times during the trial and I couldn't see much of the courtroom. What I did notice was that Bailey, Shenton and the other defendants had virtually no security compared to me and it fuelled my delusion that I really was the fucking business.

It was during this trial that I gained my reputation as a dangerous gunman, mainly due to the testimonies of several policeman. Detective Inspector Ingham, one of the main officers involved in the case and the most objective and professional policeman I have ever met, was questioned thoroughly on what he thought of me.

"Do you consider Frank Cook to be a dangerous man?" the prosecutor asked him.

"Yes," he replied, "I think Frank Cook is dangerous. He is one of the most dangerous gunmen in South Yorkshire, if not the whole country."

"Do you think he would have shot you?" Without malice, he said,

"Yes, I unequivocally believe he would have shot me, if he had been given the chance."

The judge, Mr Justice Beer, was a fair man, respected throughout the criminal world and he gave me a seven year sentence. I could tell by the look on his face that he did not enjoy putting men behind bars for long periods of time, but it was his duty and he did it well. He was under pressure to give me a life sentence because of various psychiatric reports made about me and the lack of regard for life I had demonstrated but, in the end, he gave me the seven years, with a recommendation that I should be psychiatrically evaluated and, perhaps, treated in a special prison called Grendon Underwood. With all that to look forward to, I was transferred to Strangeways, to start my sentence.

I arrived in Manchester late at night, amidst a sea of prison officers who kept telling me I wasn't big enough, tough enough, or old enough to be a gangster and that, although I saw myself as a rough diamond, this is where all the rough edges would be knocked off.

"We tame lions here, son," I was told, as I was marched through countless doors to the place where I was to be evaluated. One officer gave me a cold cup of tea in a plastic cup and I carried it very carefully, knowing that if I spilled a drop, I would get the shit kicked out of me. Eventually, we arrived at the segregation and punishment block, where I was to be housed.

"You'll be in good company now, you're next to Frankie Fraser. Do you know him?"

"Yeah, I know him," I lied. 'Mad' Frankie Fraser was one of my heroes. A former member of the Richardson Gang and a real old school gangster, feared and respected by the whole criminal community.

"Who's that? Who's that?" "Who's coming in?" "What's your name son?" All along the block, voices rang out. I knew they were desperate to discover the identity of the new inmate but I kept my mouth shut and went into my cell. I was wondering which side Frankie Fraser was on, when there was a bang on the side of my cell and a Cockney voice called out.

"Alright, who's that then?" I told him my name.

"Frank who? Who the fuck are you?" I told him him again and explained what I was in for.

"Okay," he said. Armed robbers were at the top of the prison hierarchy and when he heard what I did, I knew he would be satisfied. My interrogation was over and the other prisoners began to shout to Frankie, asking him who I was. He told them and everything quietened down for the night.

First thing next morning, it was time to slop out and all the inmates carried their overflowing pisspots to the toilets. I was looking out for a large, mean-looking Cockney, my mental image of the infamous Frankie Fraser, when a little pint-sized guy came shuffling in and walked straight up to me.

"You alright, mate?" he said in a thick Cockney accent. "I'm Frankie Fraser."

I could not believe that this frail, old man was one of London's most notorious gangland enforcers.

After this initial introduction, I didn't speak to him for a few weeks other than to say hello and I was just glad that I knew him and he was alright with me. During exercise, he would walk round the yard with his little entourage of friends and followers. I walked round on my own, not needing anyone else's company. One day, I saw him looking over at me and realised that this meant he wanted me to go over to him. He looked at the guys who were with him with a bored expression on his face, then he looked me straight in the eye.

"How are you today then, Frank?"

"I'm fine," I replied, wondering why he wanted to speak to me. He folded his arms, raised his chin into the air and asked me,

"Who gave you the name Frank?"

"My mam and dad," I replied.

"What right have they got to give you the same name as me?" I was stumped by this difficult question and I paused, my mind racing to find an acceptable answer. Suddenly, he burst into laughter.

"Naah, you're alright me old mate but remember, you've got the same name as me, so you've got to live up to it."

"Of course," I said, hugely relieved and pleased at this generous gesture of approval.

After that, me and Frankie spent a lot of time together, chatting and exchanging stories. I was fascinated to hear his tales of gangland London, which were still shocking, even by my standards. He would ask me questions about my life and background and I always told the truth. He seemed to know instinctively when someone was lying and he didn't like it. When he approved of what you were saying, he would nod his head and the more he approved, the longer the nod would be. I respected him and confided a lot about myself, even if I thought it was very negative. I think he respected my openness and we came to be pretty good mates.

One of the best times we had together, was that Christmas when the guards let me go into Frankie's cell for two hours before dinner. I had only got a couple of cards from Pat and Malcolm but he had a mountainous pile of mail from people all over the country.

"I'll tell you what we'll do," he said. "We'll open my mail and we can read it to each other." We sat opposite each other and began to open the letters and, on the third one, I noticed that he had a middle name.

"Francis NORMAN Fraser!" I naively blurted out. He looked up sharply.

"Why? What the fuck's wrong with that?"

"Nothing," I quickly replied, realising my mistake.

"Go on, speak up. What the fuck's wrong with it?"

"Nothing, it's just I haven't heard of a gangster called Norman before." He still wasn't happy.

"There's fucking nothing wrong with Norman. Norman was my uncle's name." Desperately backpedalling, I confessed that my middle name was Ronald.

"Ronald! That's a prick's name. The only thing you've got good with you, is that you're called Francis." I agreed and, to my relief, he immediately carried on opening the cards and letters, as if nothing had ever happened. With each one, he told me a little story and he reminded me of a child opening presents. He was one of the most vicious people I had ever met but, at that moment, I glimpsed a softness and gentleness in him, that did not often surface.

On Christmas Day, we were always treated to a turkey dinner, although 'treated' is perhaps not quite the right word. This year, I sat down to my meal, looking forward to a change from the normal filth. There were roast potatoes, vegetables, gravy but I couldn't see the turkey anywhere. I poked around on the plate with my knife and fork and eventually found the thinnest piece of processed turkey, stuck to the bottom of my plate. When I managed to scrape it off, there were only a few stringy bits left and these were so overcooked, I couldn't taste them. But it was better than what we normally got and, since it was Christmas, I didn't moan.

The last I saw of Frankie was in the exercise yard, on the morning before he was to be transferred. There was to be an inspection and the governor and chief officer had come down to watch. The chief officer had decided that the gates to the compound should be left open, a mistake which he probably regretted for a long time. Frankie walked in and grasped me firmly by the arm.

"Francis, I'm going now. Look after yourself and don't forget, always be honourable and show respect." I nodded.

"Don't join in, Frank," he said and then, suddenly, the small fifty-four year old man leapt like a kangaroo, arms outstretched and grabbed the chief officer by the throat. They rolled about the floor, Frankie holding onto the fat chief officer's throat with a vice-like grip and he looked like a rat holding onto a bulldog. In the end, a mass of guards were able to get him off by whacking him with their batons but not before he had nearly killed the chief officer.

Exercise was called off and we were taken back to our cells. I was wondering what had happened to Frankie, when I heard heavy bootfalls coming across the landing. I could tell there were loads of guards by the noise they made and they all came to a halt outside Frankie's door. When they opened it, I knew he must still be in there and, sure enough, one of the officers walked in.

"Pack your kit, Fraser, we're going." There was a long pause and I could hear the guards rattling their batons, trying to intimidate him. Then, I heard the Cockney voice that was now so familiar.

"I've got a fucking better idea, you pack the cunt!" With that, he marched out past all the officers and carried on along the landing. I watched as they trooped after him and, in his cell, I could hear the officers packing his bag.

I never saw Frankie again, although occasionally he sent a message to me through the grapevine and I sent a few back. Nowadays, I occasionally see him on television and a smile always comes to my face when I remember what an extraordinary character he was. He was one of the toughest, most honourable men I have ever met and, if he had not been on the wrong side of the law, he would have had a brilliant career in the forces, or as some sort of administrator.

Soon after Frankie left, I was put back into mainstream prison and then transferred to Liverpool. Back in Walton, I was allocated to H Wing and taken off the A list, although it was stipulated that I must have a single cell. This suited me fine, as I was not a very sociable person at the time and was happier in my own company than other people's. It also meant I had space to exercise, which was still something that occupied much of my time.

My hatred of the prison establishment had now diminished and I had no real desire to be subversive when I first entered Liverpool Prison. Unfortunately, my reputation had preceded me and the officers were convinced I was going to present a problem that had to be dealt with severely. I was constantly scrutinised and harassed by them until my venom was rekindled but, this time, I reacted more violently then ever before.

On one occasion, I was collecting my dinner, when a piece of food fell off my tray. The prison officer who was serving just laughed and told me I couldn't have another piece. Within seconds, he and two of his colleagues were covered with the rest of the food from my plate and I was placed on report.

I was on report so many times during my stay at Liverpool, that virtually all my time there was spent in solitary. In these times alone, I built up a paranoid fantasy that I would never be leaving prison, so I might as well be as destructive as possible. I vowed to wreak as much havoc as possible and, around this time, my aggressive behaviour escalated to dangerous levels.

The culmination of this unhealthy time was six weeks of rioting in reaction to a 'work to rule' policy, implemented by the officers, in an attempt to get more pay. We were not allowed showers, exercise sessions, visits to the chapel or any movement at all within the jail. Being locked up with no freedom is bad enough, but trying to survive in such inhumane conditions was intolerable. I was instrumental in inciting the rioting and smashed up anything I could lay my hands on, threw furniture out of the windows and set fire to debris which was thrown to the bottom of the prison, where the nonces were held. As the riot gained momentum, we took to stoning the officers and even the firemen trying to extinguish the fires burning throughout the prison. I thoroughly enjoyed this period of disruption and participated to the full. When it eventually quietened down, it was decided that I was displaying such a high level of violence that I should be transferred to the high security prison in Wakefield.

Wakefield nick, which had the highest concentration of lifers of any prison in Europe, was ironically situated on a road called Love Lane. It had a fearsome reputation and was known locally as 'Monster Mansion' or 'The House of Horrors'. All the seven hundred and fifty inmates were serving sentences of seven years minimum and most were extremely dangerous. I spent two and a half years there and witnessed countless acts of horrific violence and three murders.

Before I arrived, I decided that to survive I would have to become as violent and ruthless as the other inmates. Fortunately, news travels fast around the prison system and the reputation that preceded me, helped me gain some early respect. Even so, I had been put on A Wing which housed the most psychopathic prisoners and I knew there would be plenty of people who wouldn't give a shit about who I was, or what I had done.

Everyone in a prison like Wakefield is in a constant state of anxiety. You exist under the persistent threat of being killed or seriously injured. You have to assume that someone is out to get you all the time, or else you'll get caught off guard and attacked. The most vulnerable time is in the morning, when the doors are opened. This is when another inmate could sneak into your room, stab you and leave you to bleed in your bed. Most people put salt outside their doors, so they could hear footsteps, or they left something by the door, so it would make a noise if someone tried to open it. I was ready for any attackers and had knives stashed in various places around the prison where I felt an ambush would be likely.

I was still tremendously hyperactive and constantly had to work out to release my pent up energy. I spoke to the psychiatrist about this and he told me that I should try and tire myself out by doing even more exercise. The only effect this had, was of making me fitter and stronger and, ultimately, I had even more energy. With no other way to channel it, it eventually found an outlet in even more violence.

The first real incident, involved a guy on the wing called Joe, who came from Toxteth, the black ghetto in Liverpool. He was always staring at me and I thought he had some sort of problem and was sizing me up. I later found out that he was as paranoid as me and was only looking at me because he was worried about what I might do to him. Basically, I thought that we were going to end up attacking each other, so I decided to act first, before he could get me.

Before lock-up, I got one of my knives and went along to his cell and asked him what was going on.

"What the fuck do you mean, man?" he said, turning round to me aggressively. Without further hesitation, I smashed my fist into his face and, to my surprise, he fell straight to the floor. As soon as he hit the deck, I booted him in the head, then bent down and slashed him across the face. It was then that I realised that I had already knocked him out with my first punch. Suddenly, I thought I might have done more than just knock him out and that he might be dead. Inwardly, I began to panic but walked as calmly as I could to the cell of another inmate, Paddy Maguire.

I tried to get Paddy, a UDA paramilitary, to help me drag him into the showers but he advised me to leave him where he was, because nobody had witnessed the attack. Luckily, the screws never did find out but I still had to face the repercussions of this attack, which I knew would be brutal. I reckoned I would have to take out all of Joe's friends, or they would take me out, so I embarked upon a period of intense violence.

Over the next few weeks, I seriously assaulted sixteen of the fifty inmates on the wing. Some of the attacks were the result of genuine grievances but others were simply the inevitable consequence of my distorted perspective. I had decided that, as I was surrounded by animals, I would have to become an even bigger animal to survive. If I came into any conflict with another inmate, I would not hesitate in attacking him, usually with a knife. There are never fights in prison, just quick, brutal attacks and the aim is to do the most damage in the least time and this usually means stabbing someone or throwing boiling water over them.

Some people believe that you can get through prison by taking a passive stance and not offending anybody. This is complete nonsense. If you are not prepared to defend yourself with violence, you will be shamefully taken advantage of. You will be beaten, buggered, humiliated and used like a slave. At best, this might mean having to do menial jobs for other inmates but they might make you carry drugs for them, or be repeatedly gang-raped. I never let this happen to me and I never took part in it myself.

My cell was next to Paddy Armstrong's, a member of the Guildford Four, who were eventually cleared of being bombers. Although he was innocent, Paddy tried to live up to his terrorist tag, in order to survive in prison. We got on really well and I found him to be a very humourous man. He was an addictive gambler and, every Monday, he would borrow twenty pence from me to put on a horse. This money would faithfully be returned on the following Thursday, whether or not he had won.

The prison bookie was a sex offender called Reggie Chapman, known on the outside as the 'Barnsley Beast'. Although he was a nonce, he was quite prepared to admit to his crimes and would not take hassle from anybody. He was not at all like the normal conception of a sex case and was often involved in fights. He must have been quite tough because he held the prestigious position of bookmaker in what was a very tough prison. He gave good odds and always paid up on time.

Me and Paddy were both welders and one day we were welding cell doors when it suddenly occurred to me that we were both supposed to be subversives and yet, here we were, welding the very doors that kept us imprisoned. I shared my thoughts with Paddy, who immediately downed tools and walked to one of the officers and told him that we were refusing to work any more. We were put on solitary and, while we were there, we thought of a novel use for the welding equipment.

Neither of us liked bullies, so when we were put back on normal location, we decided to teach them a lesson they wouldn't forget in a hurry. When we caught someone picking on a weaker inmate, we would drag them down to the welding bay, where no screws would find us. Then we tied them to the bench and put one of their feet in a vice. By this time, the victim would be getting very frightened but this only added to the excitement of what we were doing. One of us would attach the large crocodile clip, which supplied the welding torch with electricity, to one of their toes and then give them a few blasts. They would writhe in agony as the shock passed through them but they couldn't scream because we had already gagged them. Sometimes the toe would turn black, so we named all the people whom we had tortured in this way, the black foot tribe. Eventually, the staff caught wind of our sadistic pastime and slammed us into solitary again, with threats of court appearances, if it happened again.

It was in Wakefield, that I witnessed my first homicide, along with another inmate, Francis McLow. A psychopath, called Robert Morley, killed two of our fellow inmates and proceeded to eat the brains of one of them, before the officers were able to stop him. This horrific act strengthened my conviction that I was amongst animals and convinced me that my policy of attacking before I was attacked myself, was my best guarantee of survival.

When there was a murder on the wing, a cloud of darkness descended. After a murder, we would be locked in our cells while they dealt with the body. One of the worst sounds I have ever heard, was the slithering of a body bag along the metal gangway, outside the cells. The whole wing would become silent and subdued after a killing. The extroverts would become introverts and the introverts seemed to disappear.

Some people were simply not capable of coping with the horrors of Wakefield and there were plenty of suicides. One incident that sticks in my mind, happened when I was doing my part-time job of cleaning the landing. I had been asked to go and check if a particular cell door was open, as the window was broken and the glazier needed to come and fix it. The door was closed, so I peered through the broken window and there I saw a pathetic old man, standing in the middle of the room in nothing but his grey, prison underpants, sawing away at his neck, with a jagged piece of broken glass. Blood was spraying everywhere and I just stared, shocked and unable to move. When I came to my senses, I raced down the landing, shouting to the officers.

Normally, they had to get permission to open a cell door but, thankfully, this time, one of them decided to break the rules and open it anyway. They arrived just in time to prevent the old man from killing himself and the medical staff followed soon afterwards. He managed to make a full physical recovery in hospital but we were told he had suffered a nervous breakdown. He was moved to the more relaxed setting of Rampton and I wondered why such an old man was being kept in Wakefield in the first place.

Because of my behaviour, I was in and out of solitary and it was during one period there, that I realised how disturbing the violence, back-stabbing and general lack of morality in the prison had become. It was a great relief when the psychiatrist concluded that I would benefit from a transfer to a therapeutic prison and I asked to be put on the transfer list as soon as possible.

I was put back on normal location to wait for clearance on the transfer and was once again submerged in the hostile atmosphere. Most people sought the security of gangs but I preferred to fight for myself. I knew that if I got involved in a gang I would, by nature, defend every member to the hilt and this would mean getting involved in many more incidents and I already had enough on my plate. By staying independent, I was more susceptible to attack because, if I offended one gang member, I would have the rest of them to contend with, single-handedly.

I was still awaiting transfer, when I witnessed a particularly pathetic inmate being bullied by another prisoner. Such bullying was a daily occurrence but something just snapped and I gave the perpetrator a really good kicking. He was part of a gang and, as a result, all its members turned against me. Over the next thirty-two weeks, I seriously assaulted each of the twenty inmates on one wing, all of whom were connected to the incident.

I was still convinced that I would never get out of prison, so I didn't care about the consequences of this spree of aggression and, when the prison psychiatrist, Dr Bradley, questioned me about it, during one of our monthly meetings, I was happy to own up. When he heard how severe the attacks were, he accelerated the transfer process, in an attempt to get me into another prison as soon as possible.

Once again, I found myself in solitary and, although this kept me isolated from the other prisoners for a while, it made me even nastier when I came out again. I'd stopped washing and, in a desperate display of defiance, I would fling my shit around the cell. I continued to nurture murderous fantasies, mentally rehearsing what I would do if I could get my hands on a screw or, better still, a governor. Basically, I was mad and very, very bad.

Grendon Underwood

"There's someone to see you, Cook." I sat up. Who could possibly want to see me?

The door opened and a big, jovial-looking man came striding into the room. There were six officers outside but he told them to stay put.

"This is my cell," he informed them. I found his appearance amusing but, inwardly, I was impressed at the audacious way in which he had just entered my cell when, presumably, he was aware of my reputation.

"Hello, my name is Doctor Gillett," he announced, as he stretched out his hand. "How long have you been in here?"

"About seven weeks," I told him, wondering where this conversation was leading.

"You're living like an animal. I want to see you this afternoon, so get yourself bathed and put some different clothes on." With that, he turned and left me alone once more.

I was completely shaken by this brief encounter, as even the smallest incident takes on an exaggerated significance when you have been in solitary for any length of time. But he was certainly not like all the other prison officials I had come across. I admired his balls and seeing him would at least get me out of the segregation cell for a little while. In fact, I was intrigued as to what he had to say to me.

The door opened again and my lunch was pushed through. As soon as I had finished eating, the officers came in and frog-marched me down to the shower block, where I took my first shower since I had been in solitary. I was given new clothes, although this was nothing to get excited about, as the screws made sure I got the most ill-fitting uniform they could find. I was handcuffed and taken to the hospital wing by a gang of supervisors and a dog handler. I was marched up to an office and one of the officers knocked on the door.

"Prisoner Cook here to see you, Doctor Gillett."

"Yes, bring him in," came the answer from within. I stood in the middle of the room, vacantly looking about, disorientated. He was hunched over his desk, absorbed in some paperwork and, without looking up, he instructed the officers to leave the room.

"Are you sure?" one of them asked him. Doctor Gillett slammed his pen down, sighed with mild irritation, then got up and walked past me, as if I wasn't even there.

"Can you leave the door because I don't need you here? I'll call your boss and you can go back to your duties. I'll deal with Cook and when I've finished I'll get someone to escort him back."

He sat down and invited me to sit in the chair on the opposite side of the desk. It was nailed to the floor, so I was directly across from him. He started to ask the usual routine questions about my age and the length of my sentence without once looking up from his paperwork. My gaze shifted to a broken glass window behind him and I began to toy with the idea of killing him. I already had more respect for him than for any of the other screws but my hatred of authority was so great, that this wasn't enough to quell my murderous thoughts. Trying to ensure that he couldn't see me looking around, I calculated that in two leaps I could jump onto the desk, then onto the window, where I could grab the glass and go for the doctor. If I didn't kill him, I could take him hostage and then take it from there. Suddenly, Doctor Gillett calmly glanced up from his work, across the desk.

"I wouldn't do that, if I were you. I've lived a very full and happy life and I'm not really worth it, I'm only here to help you," he said and then carried on with his paperwork, completely unruffled.

"Shit, he can read my mind," I thought to myself. I was really freaked out and all thoughts of attacking him immediately evaporated. I concentrated hard on flowers, fish and chips, anything; hoping he wouldn't be able to see the murderous thoughts in my head.

Eventually, he put his pen down, leant back in his chair and looked me straight in the eye.

"Does the length of your sentence bother you?"

"No."

"What are you in for?"

"Firearms offences, GBH, that sort of thing," I told him.

"And does that bother you?"

"No, not really."

"Have you got a girlfriend?"

"No, I destroy every relationship I have. You can't have relationships with my lifestyle."

"You look quite a fit, healthy, man. Do you walk round the wing, posing?"

"No."

"I see your shirt collar is buttoned up to the top. Don't you want to expose anything about yourself?"

"No, I don't feel the need to, I know what's underneath. Besides, I'd feel embarrassed."

"What do you keep your cell on normal location like?"

"There's not much in it but I keep it clean and tidy."

"My report suggests you are fastidiously tidy. Is that important to you?"

"I like to keep it smart, yes."

"And how often do you shower?"

"When I'm not in segregation, twice a day."

"I see," he said, rubbing his chin thoughtfully.

"So here we have a young man, who doesn't mind being in jail, the fact that he has tried to kill people doesn't bother him and when someone tries to love him, he destroys the relationship because it doesn't fit in with his lifestyle. He has an excellent physique but buttons his collar up to the top and he has to keep his cell clean and tidy."

He looked at me and I just shrugged.

"Frank, I haven't even asked you any questions about your mental state but the little you have told me is quite worrying. I'd like you to come to my prison."

"Yeah, I'll go," I told him.

"You'll be moved very quickly, in fact, almost straight away."

"That's okay. The only thing I want, is to be moved back on to normal location. Will you ask for me?"

I wanted him to make the request because, if I was let out for good behaviour, I would lose face amongst the other prisoners. I didn't really want to go to another prison, just to get back on the wing where I could start causing trouble again. The staff came to collect me and as I was carted out, Doctor Gillett called after me,

"See you soon, Frank."

When I got back to the wing, it was already teatime, so I ate and then went straight up to my cell. When I lay down, I realised how drained I was and instantly fell asleep. In the morning, I went down to breakfast, which was porridge as usual with a boiled egg and two slices of bread. During breakfast, I was debating whether to go to work or not. I still hadn't made my mind up when I got back to my cell, so I lay around for a bit, still thinking. I'd just decided to go to work when the door was opened and four prison officers came in.

"Pack your kit, you're going," barked one of them.

"Where to?" I asked.

"You'll find out when you get there."

After I had packed my gear, I was handcuffed and marched out of the prison and put into a van.

I had no idea where I was being taken. I knew about most of the high security prisons in Britain, so I thought I'd be able to work out our destination by ascertaining the direction in which we were heading. We went through Lancashire, so I ruled out Gartree or Long Larton. We passed through the Midlands and then on towards London. I figured we were heading for the infamous Parkhurst on the Isle of Wight but, in Buckinghamshire, we headed off into the countryside and the staff became animated and jovial. I was tense and nervous after the long journey and thought they were deliberately trying to piss me off. Then we arrived.

"Here we are Frank, Grendon Underwood Psychiatric Prison," announced one of the officers, almost gleefully.

"Oh fuck!" I thought to myself. "I've really reached the end of the line now." Grendon was a prison for the criminally insane and it hit me that I might never see the light of day again, if they didn't want me to. This was so devastating that I was literally stunned and, as they let me out of the van, my normal reaction to difficult situations was replaced by a sinking feeling and tears, painfully pricking my eyes.

Through my tears, I could make out the prison's beautiful grounds; a million miles away from the gravel exercise yards I was used to. Doctor Gillett was there to meet me with a prison officer called Ted Cole.

"I'm sorry it had to be this way, Frank, but it really is for your own good," apologised Doctor Gillett. "Anyway, you'll find out what I mean in time. Welcome to Grendon."

I was in a trance-like state, unable to comprehend that I was now considered to be mad. The thought that I had become like my mother was too hard to take in.

"Can you get him washed, changed and transferred straight to the hospital wing?" he asked the officers. This was not the normal policy, as new inmates usually went first onto an induction wing but I later found out that my case was considered extremely urgent.

On the hospital wing, Doctor Gillett instructed the escorting officer from Wakefield to take off my handcuffs.

"Are you sure? He can be very dangerous."

"We don't use handcuffs in this prison, so take them off," he insisted. A senior officer from Grendon came over and introduced himself as Peter Bell.

"I'll be looking after you," he told me. He pointed over to a room next to the office. "Your cell is over there, number thirty-nine. What diet do you want?" he asked me. I was still in a state of shock and to be given a choice of food, after years of being fed the usual prison shite, was just too overwhelming.

"Are you vegetarian?" I just nodded my head, hoping the ordeal would soon be over.

I was told to go over to the hot plate where all the other inmates were queuing for their meals. Only one member of staff was supervising mealtime but what surprised me even more, was how warm and friendly the inmates were. I had been expecting the normal cold, hostile prison welcome but these men were friendly and actually made an effort to talk to me. I was glad that I didn't have to try and prove myself but their welcome did nothing to alleviate the depression I was feeling. I normally devoured every scrap of food on my plate but I could only manage half the dinner. I put the food back on the hot plate and sloped back to my cell, to try and gather my thoughts.

I had hardly been in my cell for more than a few seconds, when there was a knock on the door and a very strange-looking lad walked in, carrying a hefty bible in his hand.

"Hello, my name's Isaac," he said.

"Alright," I mumbled and told him that I was unpacking my kit. I had expected him to walk away at this point but he continued to walk into my cell. I was very wary of people encroaching on my territory and, as a rule, never let anyone into my cell, so the situation became quite tense. Unperturbed, he started quoting from the bible and telling me about God's forgiveness and love and all that sort of thing. He was really starting to get on my nerves and I was rude and off hand with him.

"Listen," he said, "I can see you're not interested but that doesn't matter, I can save you another day but do you know how many people die of lung cancer a year?"

I had noticed a brush in the cell and had been considering threatening him with it to get rid of him but when he came out with that, I immediately thought of my mum and flipped. I grabbed the brush and smashed it over his head. I booted him out of the cell and slammed the door so hard, that the little flap in the top half fell down.

Isaac was writhing around on the floor outside my cell in agony, clutching his bleeding head and the commotion attracted the other inmates. He started to stagger to his feet and began telling me that he forgave me and that I should come out. Amazingly, the others were also reassuring me that they understood how I felt and that I should come out and talk about it. I thrust the brush pole through the bars, jabbing furiously at them to try to get them to go away.

"Fuck off, you're all fucking nuts and I don't want be here," I shouted at them. By now, Doctor Gillett and the staff had turned up and were trying to coax me out. I jumped on the bed, screaming to Doctor Gillett,

"Get me out of this fucking loony bin, I shouldn't be here, take me back to a normal prison."

"Come out and we'll sort it out," he said calmly.

"Fuck off, you're a bigger fucking nutter than any of them."

"Have it your own way then," he said and told everyone to go back to their cells, finally leaving me alone.

About an hour later, Doctor Gillett turned up outside my cell.

"Have you calmed down yet, or are you still upset?" he asked. I was feeling quite deflated and didn't even answer him. He came in anyway and, again, I was impressed by his audacity. He didn't even bother to put the latch on the door, which meant I could lock him in. He sat on the bed beside me and just said,

"You just get your head down and we'll come and see you tomorrow." I felt embarrassed and confused but there was something about his manner and his voice, which made me feel I could trust him.

Doctor Gillett said I had to stay on the hospital wing for a while, before I could be admitted to normal location and although I was not happy there, I didn't cause any more trouble. The hospital wing contained some severely disturbed people, who I didn't want to mix with, so I stayed in my cell most of the day, working out and only coming out to shower. Eventually, I did venture out a little more, occasionally making a cup of tea or some food or taking exercise in the outdoor compound. Various members of the prison staff came to visit me, some to evaluate me and others to see if I wanted to be placed on their wings.

A woman called Kate Davis, from D Wing, came to visit me and I quickly identified her as someone who could easily be manipulated. I told her that Doctor Gillett wanted me stay on the hospital wing and that it was making me unhappy. She said she would see what she could do and, sure enough, I was promptly moved to D Wing.

Here, just as in the hospital, the inmates were friendly and very talkative. The atmosphere was casual and everyone seemed very happy. It was a million miles away from the harsh regimes, violence and mass paranoia that I had experienced in every other prison and it was completely unsettling at first. I was so used to confrontation that when people were pleasant to me, it was actually very disturbing. I wanted to hate them so that I could justify being confrontational. I was comfortable with hostility but there was none at Grendon and it felt like there was a void in my life.

My therapy was due to start in a week but, before that, I was scheduled to attend a group meeting on the Friday, to help me prepare for it. I was put into Group One with ten other people and there were five groups altogether. In my group, there was another armed robber, two rapists, two arsonists and two drug addicts. Before the meeting, all the groups and all the staff from the wing, had one big meeting to discuss any wing issues or group feedback. After that, we split up into our groups and dispersed to different rooms. Before the meeting got underway, we all had to introduce ourselves and say what we were in for. For the rest of the meeting, we were allowed to ask each other whatever questions we wanted. Fortunately, nobody asked me anything and the meeting finished without event.

When I got back to my cell and reflected on the meeting, I was surprised at how apprehensive I had been and the anxiety I had felt as I wondered whether someone would ask me a question. I worried about whether I could last the therapy out. I decided to stick with it but, if anyone put any pressure on me to do something against my will, there was no way I was going to stand for it.

On normal location, I began to make friends with a lot of people and found that most of them were nothing like me. The prison was full of relatively nice lads, who weren't criminally-orientated but had simply committed a small crime. When they got into the state system and were found to have some sort of mental illness, they were assumed to be dangerous and locked away indefinitely. In my opinion, I was a professional crook, who was having a few mental problems and had little in common with these men. Even the more serious cases such as the sex offenders and arsonists were not in the same class as me.

The meetings continued, once a week and the other inmates were keen to get involved in the therapy. The ones who really took it seriously were nicknamed 'theraputons' but I certainly wasn't one of these. I stubbornly remained silent in the meetings but was quite content to listen to the other blokes moaning on about their problems and hang ups. At the start of one meeting, I noticed that the atmosphere was more tense than usual and nobody would make eye contact with me. The officer asked if anyone would like to start and a black lad called Noel, who was a rapist, put his hand up.

"I've got something to say in front of the group about Frank Cook," he said timidly. This caught me off guard. I racked my brains, trying to think how I could have offended him. I hadn't had any aggro with him and I wasn't racist. In fact, I couldn't remember even speaking to him. He was a sex offender and people like me didn't talk to people like him. He carried on:

"Frank, I'd like to say that I'm very intimidated by you." Not being the most sensitive of people at the time, I thought he was insulting me and felt like jumping up and bashing him there and then. The officer encouraged the other prisoners to speak up and, one by one, they came out of their shells and began to tell me how aggressive I was, how frightening and how unapproachable. I was feeling confused and more than a little hurt by this point. After all, I hadn't attacked anyone on the wing. To me, they were just a dirty bunch of sex cases and pricks and they thought that by playing these little games, they would somehow get parole. I wanted to tell them that all the weird things they talked about were being noted down by the authorities and would probably be used to keep them in prison but I held back – they weren't worth it anyway.

The officer asked me if I'd like to know why the other inmates were intimidated by me and I told him I would. They went on about my crew cut hair, my muscles, the way I walked, the way I talked, and the gestures I used when I spoke. By the end of the meeting, I was totally baffled. Although I had wanted confrontation over the last few weeks, I had managed to be very restrained. How could my mere presence on the wing have upset these men so much?

In the evening, the other armed robber from the group, a guy called 'Midlands' Bill, joined me in my cell for a cup of hot chocolate. He was the only one whom I felt I could relate to and I didn't mind him coming in. I asked him what he thought about what was said in the meeting, confident he would say they were all talking bollocks. But he said I should try and think about my image and the way I looked to other people. He suggested growing my hair a bit, walking instead of marching and not building my muscles so much, as these were the things that seemed to intimidate people. He appreciated that it would be difficult for me to see this, so he said he would get hold of a video camera and film me being interviewed by him. I agreed to this, so later that night, he got hold of a camera from the staff and we made a tape.

To my surprise, when I saw the tape, I could see exactly what he was talking about. It was quite shocking to see how I spoke in short aggressive bursts, pounding home my words with forceful gestures. A smile rarely graced my lips and it was easy to see how people found me very difficult to deal with.

The tape had highlighted many of the problems that had led to my being sent to Grendon but recognising them and solving them are two very different things. If anything, the tape just served to disturb me more, as I now had a clear insight into the nature of some of my problems but felt powerless to do anything about them. The pain I was feeling was becoming unbearable and, inside me, the pent up aggression I was trying to restrain, was building up to a point where something had to give.

Some of the inmates on another wing had brewed up some prison hooch and, quite by accident, I stumbled on them, as they were about to drink it. They were eager for me to join them, not through generosity, but so that I would then be implicated and couldn't grass them up. I had no intention of grassing on anybody, but they were so insistent that, even though I didn't drink at the time, I decided to have a drop and then leave.

When I tasted the 'Chateau Grendon' brew, I found it pretty good and what was more, I started to feel relaxed and happy for a change. One glass led to another and, pretty soon, I was getting a bit merry but also slightly worried that the screws would smell the potent stuff. Me and Midlands Bill decided that we should buy some of the hooch and take it back to our own wing. For half an ounce of tobacco, we got a bucketful of the stuff and quickly sneaked it back to my cell.

We needed to involve other members of the group in our little plan, so they would be equally guilty, and therefore invited two of the lads into the cell. I accepted the necessity of this plan but was far from happy about it. I was acutely aware that I was starting to relax and become absorbed into this prison's unique culture, which would make me an easy victim if I went back to a normal prison. But I was pissed and just tried to put it to the back of my mind and enjoy the hooch. We should have expected it but, in our drunken state, it came as quite a surprise, when the group officer turned up at the door and caught us red-handed. He entered the cell and my drunkenness immediately turned to hostility. I was also embarrassed that he had found me socialising with the other members of the group, so I jumped up and squared up to him.

"Why don't you fuck right off?" I snarled at him.

"No," he said and stood his ground. So I grabbed him, manhandled him out of the cell and slammed the door behind him.

"Who's up for a kick-off, 'cos they'll be coming to get us?" I asked the lads. The supposedly-tough Bill and one of the other lads, promptly got up and walked out, abandoning me with a pathetic-looking sex offender called Philip Hughes. When the screws returned with shields and came down heavy on us, we started a small-scale riot, throwing anything we could lay our hands on at them and generally going wild. Philip was a nonce, with credibility levels below zero but I was impressed at how brave and loyal he was, during our little battle.

In the end, we were hopelessly outnumbered and we got split up. I decided to surrender and let them take me to the hospital wing. I demanded that a particular guard take me there, knowing that he was the weakest. On the way there, he was so nice to me, that I started to become suspicious but I acted soberly and didn't offer him any resistance.

We reached our destination and he opened the door. Out of the corner of my eye, I suddenly noticed the peak of an officer's cap, then another, then another. I had been tricked. The door slammed behind me and I was faced with a mass of officers, all ready to jump on me. I grabbed a coffee table and launched it at them, knocking some of them to the ground and then went absolutely crazy. I was a ball of aggression, spitting, kicking, punching and destroying everything in sight. One officer managed to throw me to the floor but, as he tried to pin me down, his lighter fell out of his pocket and I sparked it in his face. He leapt up screaming and I started laying into them again and ripping off some of their shirts. I was amazed when they opened the door and sprinted for the exits.

Now, there were only the hospitalised inmates left on the wing and they had sensibly locked themselves in their cells, when they saw me coming. In the next few minutes, I rampaged round the wing, destroying everything I could lay my hands on. Then, the real effects of the hooch took hold and I suddenly felt sick and exhausted. I started vomiting violently and dragged myself into a cell and slumped onto a mattress. I intended to keep an eye out for the officers who were sure to come back when they realised my frenzy had subsided but I drifted off into a drunken state of semi-consciousness.

"The bastard's asleep." The cell door banged open and an officer darted in and jabbed me in the neck with a needle. I collapsed on the floor and didn't wake up for three days.

When I finally came round, I felt cold, stiff and wet. I had pissed myself quite a few times and my face was covered with a scruffy beard. I quickly realised that I was in a strip cell. The door opened and a frail old lady, wearing a nurse's uniform, stepped in.

"What have you been up to, eh?" she asked me, in a patronising voice. I couldn't believe that this woman had been sent to deal with a dangerous prisoner.

"Let's get you up and bathed," she said, helping me up and leading me gently into the bathroom. The sedatives had still not worn off and I felt faint and weak. She ran a bath and told me to take my clothes off. I did feel slightly embarrassed but in my current state, I was not going to argue.

There I was, sitting in a bath like a baby, while a female nurse washed me all over. It was exactly like being in a children's home again and, if I had not been so drugged, I would never have let it happen. She kept going on at me, telling me what a silly boy I'd been, what trouble I'd caused and asking me why I did it. I just sat in the bath feeling dazed and deflated.

After the bath, she gave me some pyjamas and arranged for a cell to be prepared. She made me get into bed, tucked me in and patted my head.

"You just stay there and I'll get the doctor to come and see you," she reassured me before leaving.

Before long, Doctor Gillett arrived and, as soon as he walked into the cell, I leapt out of bed.

"Sit down, Frank," he said, in his normal firm, but kind, voice. I did as he said and he came and sat on the bed next to me.

"Do you know you've injured thirty-two of my staff, seventeen of them seriously?" I just shrugged and shook my head. I was feeling confused and depressed and the last thing I needed was a lecture.

"What are we going to do with you, Frank?" he asked me, with a sigh.

"Look," I told him, "I can't remember everything I did but I'll assume the worst. Give me the stiffest penalty you can and send me back to Leeds or Wakefield, I just can't cope with the staff and everyone being nice to me. Throw me in solitary and let me stew in my own juice."

Slowly shaking his head, he looked at me, searchingly and said,

"I accepted you into this prison against the wishes and advice of every other member of staff. They said you were too dangerous for the regime here but I'm determined to help you to get over your problem. I told them I'd tame the wild Frank Cook and that's exactly what I'm going to do." He put his arm around my shoulders and I burst into tears.

I sobbed and sobbed like a child, not knowing why I was doing it, or how I could stop. It felt as if years of lost emotion were suddenly flooding back. Doctor Gillett kept his arm around me, squeezing my own arm from time to time. When I eventually calmed down a bit, he told me to get into bed and have some rest. He was going to start individual therapy with me the next day, something that was not really supposed to be part of the Grendon regime.

For the next six weeks, I could not stop crying. It was as if I had finally discovered an outlet for all the pain inside me.

My behaviour had upset the inmates on D Wing so much, that Doctor Gillett made me stay on the hospital wing while I had my therapy. I wasn't very forthcoming and Doctor Gillett, who was normally so patient and cheery, began to get frustrated. One day, he asked me why I wouldn't tell him certain things and would only skirt over important parts of my life. I told him that I was frightened that he might be compiling a dossier, which could be used to put me into a secure mental institution like Broadmoor. I feared that even if he didn't try to do this, the dossier would be kept and used against me at a later date.

He gave me his word that he had no intention of sending me anywhere like Broadmoor and that he would never pass my file onto anyone else, as he appreciated how much this would damage me. He then asked if I would be willing to start talking to him properly the next day. I trusted his assurances, so I agreed to fully engage in the therapy programme.

It wasn't out of a desire to reform that I took part in the therapy but because I wanted to discover the real reasons behind my behaviour and try and find out who Frank Cook really was. At each session, Doctor Gillett would show me new ways of looking at my life, how to analyse my actions and understand why I felt certain things. At the end of each meeting, he would leave me with something to think about, to keep me occupied until the next time we met.

I was Doctor Gillett's special case and he broke many of the prison's rules in helping me. I shouldn't have been on the hospital wing when I wasn't ill, or had individual therapy and I was viewed with resentment by many of the staff. If it hadn't been for their great respect for Doctor Gillett, who knew all his staff by name, I don't think I would have received the amount of attention I needed.

I also grew to greatly respect Doctor Gillett and looked forward to my meetings with him. I worried when he was not in the prison but felt comforted when I knew he was. I divulged everything about myself and it was the most painful thing I have ever done. Inevitably, the nature of our meetings meant that my relationship with Doctor Gillett was far closer than is usual between a governor and a prisoner. As I learned to feel emotion for the first time, I realised how important Doctor Gillett had become to me. He became like a father and he was the first human being I have ever loved.

After months of therapy, it was finally decided that I was ready to go back onto normal location. Although my meetings with Doctor Gillett had helped me, I was still nowhere near better and, as soon as I got back on the wing, I began causing trouble. Deep down, I felt like I wasn't being punished sufficiently for my crimes and still craved hostility and confrontation. I became infuriated when my constant attempts to provoke the staff all failed and, once again, I felt a rage building up inside me which, depressingly, would soon be released in the only way I knew.

I went on another mad rampage but this time there was no booze to blame; just sheer, uncontrolled violence. I managed to take a chief officer hostage and barricade myself in his tiny office. I wrapped his telephone cord tightly round his neck and told him he was a prisoner of the South Yorkshire Republican Army. Then I called the police, to tell them what I was up to and introduced them to my hostage.

To be honest, I didn't really know what I was going to do next and, as I thought about my next move, the officer started to talk to me. I was taken in by him and began to think that he actually sympathised with me. Obviously, he was just saying it to try and calm me down but I believed him and, for a split second, I lost my concentration and loosened my grip on the telephone cord. In an instant, the door flew open and another officer burst in, brandishing a huge needle. He tried to plunge it into my neck but I managed to grab his arm and turn it back on him. As we struggled, another officer ran in, grabbed the needle and injected it straight into my neck. I flew up into the air, arms flailing everywhere and then crashed straight to the floor, in a heap.

I woke up a week later and have never been the same since. I have caused problems since then, but I have never been so relentlessly hostile as I was then. All the therapy seemed to have finally had some effect and I slowly began to appreciate the results of my violence. For the first time in my life, I began to think about other people and their feelings and the consequences of my actions.

Philip, the young sex offender who had stood by me during my drunken rampage, was one of the first people to benefit from my changed personality. He was a hunchback, nicknamed 'Quasi' by the other inmates. He looked a real mess and often got picked on. I arranged for him to have physiotherapy on his back to get it straightened out, encouraged him to see the dentist and helped him to smarten himself up. His self-image began to improve and he quickly transformed himself into a completely new character. When he left prison, he found a wife and had two kids and I like to think that I played a small part in his rehabilitation.

Helping Philip gave me a real sense of self-worth and, somehow, addressing his problems gave me more insight into my own. I was making progress but, in the back of my mind, I always knew that, no matter how hard I tried, when I got out of prison, I would end up involved in crime again. All thoughts of being a professional gangster were now gone but I still saw nothing wrong with less violent forms of dishonesty. The real difference was that I actually wanted to become respectable. I had dreams of getting a regular job and having a wife and kids and, although I might have to remain a crook for a while, it was not my goal in life anymore.

Around this time, a nun called Sister Gail, who visited the prisoners in Grendon, took an interest in me. I think she wanted to try and understand my personality and try and sort me out but I was far from ready. One day, she gave me a potted plant to put on my window sill and then said to me,

"Frank, receive this young man and for every teardrop you spill whilst here with us at Grendon, this dear little plant will blossom, as your heart will, for you are not the tough guy you see yourself to be. I have picked this plant for you because you are my favourite inmate, I will watch you both grow."

I suppose she thought that accepting the plant would signify my willingness to change but I was not ready to make such a commitment, so, as soon as she left, I threw her plant out of the window. When she found out, she promptly replaced it with another and, although I can't say it really helped me, it was very encouraging to see that somebody actually cared about me.

My behaviour had improved so much by this point that I was granted two home leaves. The first one went without incident but, on my second leave, I decided to go to London. Everything was going fine until I got to the tube station. I started to worry about being late for Doctor Gillett and began to panic. I got so overwhelmed by the hustle and bustle of the underground that I couldn't read the timetable properly and ended up looking for a policeman. When I eventually found one, he was very helpful and put me on the right train and I managed to get back in time.

At the time, I didn't see the funny side but, looking back, I found it amusing that there was Frank Cook, normally running away from policemen, desperately trying to find one to help him. Anyway, these home leaves demonstrated to the staff that I could cope with civilian life and proved they were right to put their trust in me.

The end of my sentence approached and I was filled with enthusiasm as to what life on the outside held for me. Doctor Gillett shared in my excitement but it was painfully clear to both of us that I was far from better and still suffered from many psychological problems.

Before I left, I was given a full psychological analysis and the results were deeply disturbing. Although I had improved since being in Grendon, my levels of paranoia, hypomania and hostility were still off the scale. I was not exhibiting the outward signs of aggression anymore but the potential to be very violent was still lying dormant within me. Doctor Gillett said the analysis showed that I was just about ready to start a course of therapy and yet I was leaving.

Grendon helped me a lot and, if I had not gone there from Wakefield, I am certain that my behaviour would have either led to me killing someone or to getting killed myself. In the safe and stable environment of the prison, the therapy had seemed to be working and I was able to make progress, but that was an artificial situation and the real world was a different prospect altogether. I soon found myself back in Doncaster, living in the same area, mixing with the same people and suffering from the same old problems.

I was thirty years old, I had no money to support myself and, as an ex-con with no training whatsoever, I had little chance of finding conventional employment. I did make an effort to get a normal job but, after weeks of trying with absolutely no success, I found myself slipping back into crime.

Jacky

Among the people of Doncaster, there were very evident divides between those who hero-worshipped me, those who feared me and those who hated me. I found it much more difficult to fit into the community than I had expected and nobody seemed prepared to believe that I had actually changed. The police were especially sceptical and were constantly watching and harassing me. I know I had committed crimes in the past, but their assuming I was guilty of virtually every crime in the town was not helpful to my plans to reform.

These were huge problems that I needed to deal with but, closer to home, there was an even more pressing dilemma. After my release, I had gone to live with my cousin Malcolm and his family. Malcolm, once the fearsome leader of the Firm, had now done his time for his part in the gang warfare and had become a Jehovah's Witness. He was ultra-religious and constantly tried to force his new-found beliefs down my throat. I couldn't cope with this kind of pressure and, one night, I told them I was going to the pub but never returned.

Unfortunately, although I was now free from my devout cousin, I was also in breach of my parole conditions and Malcolm was quick to do the Christian thing and inform the police. I was unlawfully at large and didn't have anywhere I could tell the parole officer was my new home. I was sleeping with various young women in the area and staying at their houses but I knew this could only be a temporary arrangement and I was looking for a permanent solution.

Very quickly, I got bored with just going to the gym every day and I needed other activities to fill my time. Although I had not drunk for years, I found myself spending a lot of time in pubs for the social aspect, rather than the alcohol. After being in prison for a long period, you are keen to meet normal people and basically just enjoy some conventional relationships. Unfortunately, the people I ended up chatting to tended to be all my past criminal associates and they were constantly encouraging me to do jobs with them.

In a nightclub, one evening, I met a woman called Jacky, who turned out to be the answer to both my accommodation and employment problems. She was very tall, with a marvellous figure and lovely red hair. I thought she was gorgeous and very charming but this was hardly surprising, after the amount of time I had spent in prison. I ended up sleeping with her and, after I had explained my situation, she said I could stay in her flat.

The following day I phoned my probation officer and said I would tell him where I was staying, as long as he guaranteed that I wouldn't be sent back to prison. He agreed and I went down to the probation office and logged in my new address.

Living with Jacky was superb. Her flat was comfortable and filled with all the mod-cons, she cooked wonderful meals and we had great sex. The only thing that puzzled me was how she got all her money but, as life was so good, I didn't worry about it for a while. I suppose it should have been obvious, but I was quite surprised to discover that Jacky had a very lucrative job as a prostitute.

The fact that she was a 'working girl' in itself did not discourage me but I was concerned that people might think I was her pimp. After all, she often gave me money and people knew that I had no means of income. I thought long and hard about the matter and it concerned me that Jacky and other girls like her from the area, were often bullied and attacked by the pimps and punters who they dealt with. When Jacky asked my advice on this problem, I resolved how I could prove myself and make a bit of money into the bargain.

There were thirteen women working the local patch and I summoned them all to gather in Jacky's flat to hear my plan. I promised them, that if they gave me just ten pounds of their night's earnings, I would provide them with the best security service money could buy. There was much debate and haggling but, in the end, they unanimously agreed to take me on to protect them. I now had a new job and wasted no time in getting down to work. That same night, I went down to the Broxholme Lane area of Doncaster and walked round the streets, assessing the situation.

When I had singled out my targets – the pimps, drug pushers and bullies – I told them that their activities had to stop immediately, or they must face the consequences. The sale of drugs, especially, had to cease, as this would then give the police little reason to come into the area and would leave the girls free to work in peace. Even though the lowlifes whom I targeted didn't doubt that I was capable of carrying out my threats, they thought I had gone crazy. After all, I was a gunman and armed robber, not someone who would be involved with prostitutes. They should have heeded my warning, because the next night I returned and made good my threats.

For a mere fifty pounds, I was able to hire a vanload of racist thugs and neo-Nazi skinheads who I drove down to Broxholme Lane. Then, all I had to do was open the van doors and unleash the maniacs onto to the largely ethnic group of pimps, pushers and bullies, whom I had spoken to the night before. To say there was utter carnage would not be an exaggeration and my men performed their task with ruthless efficiency. Needless to say, the next evening, the area was free from the 'undesirable element'. I paid the men and retained the senior members as enforcers, who would stage 'clean-up' missions from time to time.

The morality of this approach is certainly questionable, but I figured that by using scum to combat scum, I was keeping them at each other's throats and away from the general public. It may seem like an extreme solution, but the girls were not normal people, working in a normal environment, and they were extremely grateful for my intervention.

In fact, the girls became so grateful that my role became very demanding. I was seen as some kind of figurehead by them and they would not hesitate in coming to me with all sorts of problems. At the same time, I was treading a very fine line between Doncaster's criminal fraternity and the Sheffield Vice Squad, who had now started to take an interest in me. My activities earned me eleven hundred pounds every week but, perhaps more importantly, enhanced my status to the point where the Broxholme Lane area was known as my manor. I realised that, as I had now succeeded in asserting my authority there, I could afford to take a back seat. I decided to launch myself back into the nightclub scene and set off into town, in search of a door to work.

At that time, a club doorman could expect twenty quid for a night's work. Because of my reputation, greatly exaggerated by the police and their constant enquiries, my criminal record and my careful public relations, I was able to demand a fee of between fifty and sixty pounds. Although I had not yet personally engaged in any violence since leaving prison, I was still able to be so verbally and physically threatening that I never needed to. It was ironic that the more dangerous and psychopathic people believed I was, the less violent I had to be.

Jacky had given up her career as a prostitute and we moved to a private house in Balby, the area where I grew up. She had recruited a gang of female shoplifters, who operated throughout the whole of the North of England, using our house as headquarters. Shoplifting is classed as petty crime but these women were professionals and cleared out some of the biggest stores around. The stolen goods were all stored in our spare bedroom and were sold for thousands of pounds.

In the eyes of the neighbourhood, me and Jacky were the perfect modern couple. We had a nice house, a car each, we dressed smartly and were seen in all the right places. But beneath our respectable facade, we were both determined criminals. People knew about my past but Jacky had a whiter than white image and this helped her, in her shoplifting escapades.

At this point, our joint income was phenomenal. I was still earning plenty from protecting the prostitutes and working on club doors. Also, I was acting as a modern day Fagin for piss-pot burglars. Jacky had her band of shoplifters, working six days a week and they were absolutely raking it in.

The fact that all these activities were criminal and that Jacky was an ex-prostitute did not bother me in the slightest. I was doing very well for myself and we made a good team. Actually, her determination and resourcefulness as a crook often surprised me and she was a better villain than any man I had known. We often argued, physically hitting each other on many occasions, but this never affected our criminal allegiance or our appetite for sex, which played a huge part in the relationship.

A lot of my activities relied on my reputation as a hard man but I hadn't engaged in any violence since getting out of Grendon. My enemies began to realise this and I started to sense bad vibes. My entire credibility was being questioned and I felt I had to act. I needed to do something that would reassert my authority but not land me in jail if people got wind of it. I was really annoyed by the arrogance of some of these people who were going round slagging me off and what I really wanted to do was go down to town and cause them maximum damage. It took a lot of effort to control my violent urges but, in the end, I managed to come up with what I thought was a more sensible plan.

I drove down to Broxholme Lane, armed with a knife and truncheon and within fifteen minutes, a gang of young men and women approached the car. I leapt out, shouting and screaming and brandishing the knife and most of them scattered. There were four men left and I wasted no time in attacking them. Although I had my knife and truncheon, they were more for show and I didn't try to stab them at all. We fought for a while and, in the end, I came out with worse injuries than them.

Later that evening, I was arrested for the serious assault of the four men. I had done nothing more than jab them with my knife, barely breaking their skin. I looked in a worse state than them but I knew the investigation would be geared against me because of my history and the police's desire to see me go down again. They exaggerated the attack so much that I was remanded in custody for the twelve weeks preceding the trial.

The trial at Doncaster Crown Court, resulted in plea bargaining and I was given a two year probation order. The judge said he couldn't impose a custodial sentence because, although he felt I should be in the dock, he thought the four men whom I had fought should also be there. He saw how my offences had been grossly exaggerated and had no other choice but to exercise leniency in the interests of a fair trial.

Although I had escaped a jail sentence, I realised how close I had been to going back inside and decided to halt all my criminal activities immediately. Jacky was right behind me and said it wasn't worth going back to prison for anything. Money was no problem; there was plenty left over from my crimes and Jacky was still shoplifting. The idea of leading an honest, industrious, life appealed to me and we both dreamt of starting a family.

After much discussion with Jacky, I decided to set myself up as a builder. I bought a van, employed two other men and placed adverts in the paper for construction work and, before long, we were inundated with offers. I was not that good a builder but the other two were excellent and, since I was willing to work hard, things went well. I didn't really like the work but it kept the police away from my door and that was all that mattered. Occasionally, they would come round to check I was still on the straight and narrow but they never had any cause to complain.

It was difficult to adjust to this new lifestyle but I was trying hard and it seemed to be going well. Jacky was pregnant and the thought of having a baby in the house inspired me to try even harder. Unfortunately, Jacky was having difficulty adapting to our more conventional lifestyle and seemed to be uncomfortable in the settled environment of our household. Initially, I put my worries down to my insecurity and paranoia but, as time went on, it became evident that something was wrong.

I suspected she was having an affair and, although I couldn't prove it at the time, two years later my suspicions were confirmed. I suppose I was so content with the situation that I didn't want to believe she would do that to me and I convinced myself that her hostility was due to her pregnancy. I also felt that I might be the cause of our problems and made extra efforts to bring happiness into our home but these failed miserably.

Jacky went into hospital to have the baby and I was present at the birth. Beforehand, several fathers had told me that you can't imagine what it's like until you are actually there and it certainly was something new and amazing to me. Jacky gave birth to a little girl who we called Stacey and, as I saw her for the first time, all I felt was incredible flood of emotion towards all females. Afterwards, I was glad that I was a man and would never have to go through the painful ritual of childbirth.

It really overwhelmed me when I was handed my little baby daughter. She looked so healthy and I was thankful that she was a girl. It seemed like I'd finally created something worthwhile and it made me very determined to stay straight. I also realised that I was going to have to work twice as hard, now I had a baby and a wife to support. I didn't want Stacey to be exposed to any criminal behaviour and, secretly, I hoped that she just might be the thing to break the chain of criminality that had run through my family for decades. I was truly elated at my daughter's arrival.

At the beginning, Jacky was equally enthusiastic about the baby and she acted like the perfect mother. But soon it became apparent that she could simply not fit into a normal family setting. I helped with the housework and changed and fed the baby whenever I could and most mornings I would get up a six and tidy the house, before Jacky got up. On summer mornings, I would put Stacey in her buggy and go for long walks but when I returned, Jacky was usually still languishing in bed, which seemed symbolic of her refusal to accept the responsibility of bringing up a child.

I then discovered that Jacky had borne another child, the year before I got out of prison and that she had abandoned it. When I confronted her with this, I expected her to react, if not tearfully, then at least angrily but it shocked me when she showed no emotion at all. It was as if the child meant nothing to her, just something she had forgotten or left behind.

As time went on, Jacky became less and less interested in keeping the family together and her coldness towards me increased. We had violent rows and she would often attack me and, I am ashamed to say that, on two occasions I hit her back. However, the more hostile she became, the more determined I was, to make things work. I remembered my experience in Grendon and thought that, maybe if I was nice to her, no matter what she did to me, it would eventually salvage our relationship. Looking back, it was probably naive to think that anything could have saved it, as our personalities were simply too volatile.

I was still on probation and, in one of my weekly visits to my probation officer, I admitted to him that I had struck Jacky, on two occasions, with the flat of my hand. He had assured me that the meeting was in confidence and, foolishly, I believed him. I trusted him and felt the need to confide in him because of the profound shame I was feeling but he took it upon himself to go and visit Jacky behind my back.

"Leave Frank, or he will kill you," he warned her, fuelling her already fertile imagination. I was very hurt by this. I regretted hitting Jacky and I had told him about it, believing it was the right thing to do.

Very soon, we were paid countless visits by various people from the social services. I knew we had problems but I was fiercely protective of Stacey and wouldn't have seen her come to any harm. The presence of officialdom in my home was an intrusion and it only served to aggravate the domestic situation.

One afternoon, the woman from the social services even admitted to me that she considered the visits to be unnecessary. She also confided that they were purely due to the instructions of the probation officer, who considered

I might be a danger to the child. I was astounded. Yes, I was a violent man but I was not a child batterer or a nonce. This assessment of me, together with the constant barrage of criticism from Jacky, was so painful that I even started to question my sanity. For a while, I believed that everyone else knew I was mad and I just wasn't capable of seeing it myself.

By now, Jacky had convinced herself that I was actually insane and was trying to force me to accept that all our problems were my fault. I knew I was partly to blame but I was genuinely trying to sort things out, whereas she was just out to destroy me. I began to drink more, in an effort to help me relax and Jacky decided that once I had a drink inside me, I went crazy. She constantly reminded me that I had been in Grendon, a psychiatric prison and that my mother had been insane. She was so persuasive and persistent in her attempts to convince me of my madness that she nearly succeeded in sending me into mental turmoil but, one day, I managed to expose her lies.

After work, I called into the local pub but instead of ordering my usual half of lager, I took a sip of one of my mate's pints and went straight home. I was greeted by Jacky who gave me a kiss as she always did. It was not a sign of affection, but a sneaky way to smell my breath. When she smelled the alcohol, she began her usual histrionics, screeching at me and goading me, by telling me I was going mad.

"Look at your eyes Frank, you're changing. Look how ill you've become, I'll have to tell the probation officer." She ranted on but, for the first time, I welcomed the barrage of accusations. I knew I was not under the influence of alcohol and I now understood that she had been playing a cruel game, trying to undermine my confidence in myself.

Having uncovered Jacky's deceit, I decided something had to be done. She was not only a risk to me but also to Stacey and I wanted to get her out of the house for a while. It was common knowledge that Jacky was a complete slut and I planned to capitalise on this fact. I sat her down and said we needed to discuss our relationship. I went on about how things weren't working out and suggested that perhaps we should have a trial separation. I suggested that she should go on holiday and then decide whether we should struggle on like we were doing, or leave each other, on amicable terms. With that, I managed to get her on the first plane to Spain with a wallet full of pesetas.

Jacky was a slut and it was not too unreasonable to assume that once in the sun, away from me and under the influence of alcohol, she would quickly give vent to her sexual desires. In fact, I was confident that Jacky would fall for the first load of shit fed to her by some Walter Mitty medallion man and come back saying she was in love and my plan proved to be ninety-nine percent successful.

Sure enough, when Jacky returned, she told me that she had found someone else and was going to leave me but I was devastated to hear that she also intended to take Stacey with her. In one sense, I was delighted to get rid of her but the final recognition that the relationship was over and especially the loss of Stacey, depressed me greatly at the time. I was on my own and I suddenly became aware that I had little money left. All my dreams of having a normal life had been dashed and there was nothing to prevent me from falling back into my old ways.

By Christmas, I had been free and single for six weeks. I was still living in the house in Balby but it had been cleared out by Jacky, to build a home with her new man. Mortgage and insurance debts were piling up and I was inevitably becoming involved in various criminal activities. I soon realised that I would have to become far more active if I wanted to reach my previous level of financial comfort and the crime soon escalated.

I also managed to hold down various normal jobs at this time. I worked as a reception manager in restaurants and wine bars during the day, as a doorman for pubs in the early evening and, in the late evening, I would drive to Manchester to work on the door of the Hacienda nightclub. I had started to use cocaine, partly to keep up with this hectic lifestyle and partly because it made me feel so fucking good. Although nobody said it to my face, most the people I mixed with knew I was psychologically addicted to it.

At the Hacienda, I would always drink while I was working, as it seemed an inevitable part of the job. Unfortunately, one night when I was driving back, the police stopped and breathalysed me. I lost my licence and, with it, any chance of continuing with this semi-legal approach to work. The debts were still unpaid and it was obvious that I would have to increase my criminal activities even further.

I wasn't entirely happy about engaging in this increased level of crime but, in a sense, it was my real career and what I enjoyed best. Over the next few months, I embarked upon my most intense period of criminal activity ever. Apart from sex crimes and homicide, there were virtually no crimes I didn't get involved in. The main problem was that to cope with all this, I needed to take a lot of cocaine and, although becoming dependent did not particularly bother me, I was concerned at the extent of the financial drain it put on me. I was in a vicious circle of needing the drugs to work and the money from work to pay for the drugs. The more I worked, the more drugs I needed.

I had been separated from Jacky for about sixteen weeks when, out of the blue, she called me at the restaurant where I worked. We chatted about Stacey and eventually she told me that the man she had met in Spain had run away and she was going to move into a council house in Doncaster. She didn't seem in the slightest bit concerned that her relationship had failed and was excited about making a new start in a new home. After a couple of minutes, I began to wonder what my part in all this was, as we had already split up.

Apparently, Jacky felt that the council house was not good enough for her and Stacey and it would be in the interest of my daughter if I financed half the repairs that were needed to make it habitable. At first, I argued with her but I was genuinely concerned about Stacey's welfare so, in the end, I agreed. She wanted me to give her two grand and, although I didn't have the money, I knew a man who would happily lend it to me.

I wanted to view the property for myself before I poured my money into it but I had lost the address, so I decided to travel down to the area where it was situated and try and find it. As I wandered about in the rain, I caught sight of two figures in the distance. One, I immediately recognised as Jacky and the other, who was pushing a buggy, was a man I didn't recognise. I walked over, suspicious as to the identity of this man who was pushing my daughter round. Jacky introduced him as John, a "damn fine builder," and the man who would be repairing the house. This did allay my suspicions, as he didn't seem her type and, to be honest, was not a pretty sight to look at.

We made our way to the rented house and I had to agree that it was in an appalling state. Assertively, I asked John about his ability to clean the place up and the amount of money he expected to earn from the venture. After listening to his estimate and making a mental note of the materials he said he would need, we came to an amicable agreement about the amount of cash I would give him. We also agreed that I would help labour on the house, as this would save some money and show goodwill towards Jacky, which was important if I wanted access to Stacey. Within forty-eight hours, the materials were delivered and we were ready to start work.

During this time, I had in no way relinquished my criminal activities. I would work on the house in between crimes but I actually dedicated all my spare time over the next sixteen days to the repairs. Neither John nor Jacky would be present, but there would always be a list of tasks for me to perform. I must admit that I congratulated myself on this show of benevolence and hoped it would impress Jacky into letting me visit Stacey regularly.

The house was virtually finished and I was feeling rather proud of myself. It was looking really smart and it was mostly down to my hard work. I was packing up, ready to leave, when I noticed Jacky and John sauntering down the road, displaying a remarkable degree of familiarity for a builder and employer. My doubts were aroused but there was still some uncertainty in my mind, as I was aware that the enormous amount of cocaine that I was taking was making me suspicious of everbody and everything.

I went home, washed, changed and got ready for work in the pub. All the time, thoughts of Jacky's 'working' relationship played on my mind and I became more and more agitated. Finally, I decided to phone up the guest house where she was staying, hoping to get a clearer picture of her relationship with John. An old woman answered the phone,

"Hello, Guest House."

"Hello, is there a woman called Jacqueline there please? She's a tall attractive lady with a daughter called Stacey. I'm her brother and I'm trying to track her down."

"Oh, I'm sorry. She is staying here but she's not here at the moment. She's with her boyfriend, getting their house ready for the wedding."

I went on to describe John and she confirmed that he was her boyfriend. I was right, the dirty whore had taken me for a ride. I had not only paid for their little love nest but had also helped to build it. To say I was pissed off would not begin to describe my mood on receiving this information and my thoughts immediately turned to violence. Calmly, I picked up a carving knife, phoned a taxi and ordered him to take me to the house, where I expected to find Jacky and her lover.

As I strode up the driveway, my body was tingling with adrenalin-induced warmth. The thought of killing the pair of arrogant bastards comforted me. I remembered everything that Jacky had done to me in the past and quickened my step. There would be no threats, no messing about, I was going to walk in there and swiftly kill them both. My thinking was clear and level-headed and I was totally aware of what I was about to do. I was also fully aware of the possible reprisals, the probable prison sentence and even the fact that my daughter would be left without parents, but nothing was going to stop me.

I entered the house and searched every room. It was empty but this didn't deter me. I went back out to the taxi and told the driver to take me to various locations in the Doncaster area, where I suspected they would be. I was desperate to find and kill them but it felt as if they were being shielded from me. The taxi fare was huge by this point. I paid it, cursing my bad luck and reluctantly set off for work, still armed with the knife.

Over the next forty-eight hours, Jacky and John dominated my thoughts but my desire to kill them, slowly subsided. I sank from an immense high into deep depression and I felt like a broken man. Memories from childhood and my many years in prison returned to haunt me and began to gnaw at my insides. The terrible, depressing reality of recent events finally hit me and I spent the next four days at home, wallowing in self-pity.

Perhaps this was a cathartic experience, because I quickly began to perk up. I pulled myself together and started to seek out my criminal associates and carried on with my regular work. The one goal I now had, was to become very wealthy and I would stop at nothing to fulfil my ambition.

I was still working as a doorman at various nightclubs in Doncaster and this presented me with the perfect opportunity to try a new way of making money. Drugs were the order of the day and I dealt small amounts of speed and coke to customers in the nightclub. This was a useful sideline, which helped to supplement my income but the debts from the house were huge and I had to get involved with far more serious crime, if I was to have any hope of paying them off.

I was involved in armed robberies, fraud, burglaries, arson and I was constantly receiving stolen goods to sell on. I was now operating on a national scale, which meant I needed to be more ruthless than ever before. All the revenge attacks that I had previously deferred, I now carried out and, in the next sixteen weeks, I stabbed or slashed, twenty-nine members of Doncaster's criminal fraternity. I feel no remorse for these attacks, as the victims were all professional villains, just as violent as me. The only distinction between us was that I got in first.

A Grisly Discovery

Around this time, I met a woman called Elaine in a pub. She was a widow, nine years my senior. I managed to cadge a lift home in a taxi with her. She was very quiet, smart and seemed very intelligent and I was sure that if I told her the truth about myself, she would be disgusted and refuse to have anything to do with me. Instead, I pretended I was a respectable bloke and managed to charm my way into her house for coffee.

Over the next two weeks, our relationship developed quickly and Elaine invited me to move in with her. I gladly agreed to live in her large, expensive house, which had its own private estate. I got the impression that she had fallen for me in a big way and, although I liked her and thought she was a lovely person, I couldn't reciprocate such strong feelings.

What I did identify in this arrangement, was the opportunity to solve all my financial problems. I could now move out of the house I had shared with Jacky and rent it to tenants. The money I would get from them, would be enough to pay the debt off and I would finally start to make some money. The chance meeting with Elaine had turned out to be very beneficial.

This all sounds terribly mercenary, but I didn't just move in with Elaine because it would help me out. I respected her a great deal and enjoyed spending time with her and, after Jacky, it was a great relief to find a woman who cared for me and treated me well. What did concern me was that she thought I was a respectable man and I was worried that she would discover the truth. However, she was a very sensitive and understanding woman and, in the end, I decided that I would risk telling her myself.

To my surprise, she was not appalled when I told her what I was involved in and she sat and listened calmly. She told me that, although she did not approve, it did not change the way she felt about me and she still wanted me to live with her. Her understanding attitude towards me was such a contrast to Jacky's that it was almost heartbreaking. Even worse, her goodness made me realise the depths to which I had sunk but, although I was disturbed by the person I had become, I figured it was too late to change.

There was no way that I could conduct a normal relationship, whilst simultaneously keeping up my criminal activities, yet they had to continue as they were my only source of money. I also felt that, because of these crimes, it was only a matter of time before I landed back in prison. I had been out for the longest time ever in my adult life and, judging by past form, I was about ready to end up back inside. This depressing and fatalistic view of my future made me feel that it would be unfair to become to involved with Elaine, as it would hurt her when I went away and also make prison more difficult for me if I was missing her.

I had rented the house to an ex-convict who had just been released from Hull Prison and two of his mates. He was still involved in theft, which was useful, as I could buy the spoils of his crimes and sell them on to make money. They weren't the best tenants and didn't always pay the rent on time, but I was happy to have the responsibility of the house off my hands.

After a few months of living with Elaine, a job came up which I couldn't refuse. For two-hundred and fifty pounds, a group of lads wanted me to me to drive them down to London and back. I didn't have to get involved in any criminal activities and I chose not to ask what they were up to. Later, I found out that the boot was full of drugs but, at the time, although I was perfectly aware that they would be involved in some sort of illegal activity, I had no idea what it was.

We stopped in Harrow, at the flat of a young couple who the lads knew. I asked if I could go back to Doncaster and pick them up after the weekend but they wanted me to stay, in case they needed driving to other parts of London. I spent the weekend sitting around in the flat, watching television, or at the pub over the road, chatting to one of the lad's wives.

On the Sunday evening, the lads returned in an elated mood, carrying bundles of money. We agreed to go for a drink in the pub, have a spliff and then go home. It was my round, so I ordered the drinks and, while the barmaid was pouring them, I nipped to the loo. When I got into the toilet, a strange feeling that something terrible had happened came over me. I made my way back to the bar, so shaken up by this feeling, that one of the lads asked me what was the matter. Without thinking, I blurted out that we must return to Doncaster immediately, because something dreadful had happened.

Although they thought I had freaked out and started moaning, eventually the lads agreed to leave their drinks and return home. We sped along the motorway and the nearer to Doncaster we got, the more agitated I became. I started to sweat and, in the pit of my stomach, I sensed something awful had happened. The other lads didn't share my anxiety but I could tell that, although they would never admit it, they were glad to be going home as well, after the long weekend.

When we got to Doncaster, I was in quite a state and, because of my feelings of foreboding, I persuaded the lads to come round to the house I rented, to check if everything was alright. When we got to the house, 58, Regent Street, Balby, I wouldn't park next to it and, instead, pulled up across the road.

"Someone go and have a look," I suggested.

"Why don't you go, Frank? It's your fucking house," replied a lad called Grovesy, who was starting to get pissed off with me. I told him there was no way I was going in there on my own, which annoyed him even more.

"Give me the fucking keys, I'll go. You're off your fucking head, you," he sneered at me. I took the house keys off my ring, not wanting to take the car key out of the ignition and handed them to him.

Grovesy got out of the car, slammed the door and stormed over to the house. I locked the door after him, started the engine and put it into gear. I watched nervously as he opened up the house, switched the light on and walked upstairs. I heard him banging about, looking in the rooms and then the light came on in the bedroom. Within seconds, it went off again and I heard him come hurtling down the stairs.

I didn't know what he had found but it was obviosuly something pretty bad. I quickly unlocked the door and revved the engine. Grovesy came sprinting out of the house and, within a flash, he was in the car alongside me, breathing heavily. Without saying a word, I put my foot down hard and we sped away through the darkened streets.

When we were a fair way from the house, I pulled the car up and turned to Grovesy.

"What's wrong?" I asked him.

"There's a dead body upstairs." I looked at the rest of them, much calmer now that my fears were confirmed.

"I told you," I said, feeling no satisfaction that I was right.

"Whose is it? What does it look like?" I questioned him.

"I don't know. He had dark hair. There was blood all over. He's had his head caved in," he blurted out.

I told them that the only lad with dark hair who lived in the flat was a kid called Andrew Sutcliffe. Although he dabbled heavily in an assortment of drugs, he was one of the nicest lads you could ever meet and the chances of someone murdering him were very remote. I figured that whoever had killed him, was actually looking for me, as I had dark hair as well. When I shared this conviction with the other lads, they naturally all wanted to be dropped off home as quickly as possible. I was shitting myself at the thought of a murderer, on the loose, looking for me and the other lads were worried because they were now connected both to me and the house. I delivered them all safely home then, despite an instinctive desire to dash off home myself, I decided to return to the house.

I had developed a morbid curiosity to go back and see the body and, eventually, I plucked up enough courage to drive to the house. I parked outside and calmly walked round to the back door, steeling myself for what I was about to find. When I opened the door, a foul stench immediately hit me but the sense of death in the house was even more overpowering. As I switched on the hallway light, I was gripped by a cold fear. I sensed that I was not alone in the house and I was painfully aware that, at any second, someone could jump out and try and kill me.

I walked up the stairs, carefully leaving all the doors wide open, so I could escape in a hurry, if necessary. I approached the bedroom, grasped the door handle, took a deep breath and very cautiously entered the room. I turned on the light and the first thing that hit me were claw marks, all over the wallpaper. The furniture was strewn everywhere and it was obvious that a fierce struggle had taken place. Everything was covered in thick, dark, sticky, blood and, underneath the overturned bed, there was a pair of feet sticking out.

Carefully, I lifted the end of the bed, to reveal Sutty's body. He was lying face down in a revolting pool of his own congealed blood and vomit. It didn't take a pathologist, to see that he'd been dead for a long time. When I turned him over, it was immediarely apparent that he hadn't been hit over the head, as Grovesy had said. It looked as if he had choked to death, probably on his own vomit.

I had known Sutty well and I had liked the lad. It was sad that he was dead, but what was more worrying, was that I would definitely be number one suspect for his murder. The situation was so ridiculous, that I found it grotesquely amusing. A smile came to my lips as I checked his body for clues to what had happened. Having found none, I turned and walked out of the door, desperately trying to remain calm. I didn't want to hurry, as this would arouse suspicion but I still felt there could be someone else in the house and I was desperate to get out.

On the way out, I made sure I rubbed off any fingerprints I had left on door handles and slipped out of the back door, making sure nobody saw me. Then, I went round to the front door and banged loudly, so the neighbours would hear. Finally, I called at the next door neighbour's and asked him if he had any idea of the whereabouts of the tenants. I left my telephone number and a message for them to contact me, as soon as possible. Satisfied that I had now adequately covered my tracks, I got back into the car and drove off as slowly and nonchalantly as I could.

I decided that, in the circumstances, it would be better if I kept a low profile for a while and there was some business in London that I needed to take care of, so I headed down south for a few days. After four days, I telephoned Elaine, who was used to my frequent disappearances by now, and she told me that the police had discovered the body and were holding me responsible. I assured her that I was innocent and told her that I would return to Doncaster immediately.

I was under no illusions that I would not be arrested eventually but felt there was no point in giving myself up. Firstly, the police knew me well and would be unlikely to believe a word I told them, so I couldn't help the enquiry. They would be very suspicious that I had come to them in the first place and it would only make my situation worse. Also, my alibi was not exactly ideal, in that I was driving a bunch of criminals around London at the time of Sutty's death. Basically, I was in for a hard time and I wanted to put it off for as long as possible.

Sure enough, I was arrested in Elaine's house and hauled down to Doncaster police station for questioning. I was suffering the comedown from weeks of cocaine and amphetamine abuse, long journeys and countless late nights and was, therefore, in a state of high anxiety. My anxiety increased as the police questioning proceeded, as I had been committing so many crimes which I obviously could not talk about. It was very difficult to construct a plausible alibi and they concluded that I was withholding information.

Ultimately, the police discovered that Sutty had died from a drugs overdose and, although they couldn't prove he was murdered, it was obvious something sinister had happened. They also found out who had been with him at the time of his death so, fortunately, I was now out of the frame. The police still suspected that I had some connection with his death and the public were certainly convinced of my guilt. I spent the next day trying to persuade people of my innocence but what bothered me the most, was the increased police scrutiny I was now going to be subjected to.

All my usual criminal accomplices suddenly vanished, the intense police surveillance was too much for them. Only a few loyal partners in crime stuck around, to help me carry on my illicit activities. These comprised a hardcore of dedicated criminals and I was glad to have them around. My reputation as a 'bad arse' was enhanced by the murder, as most people still concluded that I had killed Sutty and, although I repeatedly told them I was innocent, I was pleased by my continued ability to provoke fear.

Along with a number of my accomplices, I began my own investigations into Sutty's death and found out that the bulk of his money and all of his drugs, had been stolen. The drugs had been stolen from a chemist, so we knew what they were and it wasn't difficult to identify the pushers who were peddling them around the city centre. Even so, it was difficult to pinpoint exactly who was there at the time of his death and who had actually administered the fatal overdose.

One evening, I was in a pub in the town centre, when a pair of Sutty's mates, Hazy and Clockwork, came to see me. They were very upset and were talking about avenging his death and openly accusing the same people who we thought were responsible. After many drinks, some speed and some cannabis, I agreed to advise them on how to carry out a revenge attack. I was still worried that people thought I had killed Sutty and, after some more booze and drugs, I said I would show them the house where the main culprit lived and supply them with a gun to do the business.

We drove out to an estate in Cantley, on the outskirts of Doncaster where Bennett, the guy we were looking for, lived. After they had dealt with him, I was going to take them to all the haunts of heroin pushers in Doncaster and they could attack them as well. This would send ripples throughout the criminal underworld and instil fear into the dealers, who we regarded as scum. I accept that this appears to be hypocritical, as I was also dealing some cocaine and speed but smack was seen as the worst of all drugs and those who dealt it were scorned by most villains.

Hazy and Clockwork were reputedly a pair of super-hard thugs but when we got to the house, they were both shitting themselves. I was irritated by their pathetic behaviour but, at this point, I was emotionally worked up and high from the drinking and drug-taking, earlier in the evening. I forced Clockwork to bang on the door, which he did rather feebly, so I took matters into my own hands and grabbed the gun.

I went round to the back of the house, intending to go in there and execute Bennett where he stood but when it was clear there was nobody in, I blasted out the back windows of the house. I then gave the gun to Hazy and told him to shoot through the back door. Once he had done this, his confidence seemed to rise and he was only too eager to carry on. We went round to the front and he put a round through the door. I reloaded the single-barrelled shotgun and blasted all the front windows as well.

Clockwork, who had a reputation as a real hardman amongst the skinhead, football-hooligan fraternity, was overcome by fear and he fled into the night. Like many so-called, tough guys, he was all image, with nothing to back it up when it came to the crunch. When it was obvious that nobody was going to get killed, he came back and we all broke into the house. With great ferocity, we set about destroying the house and everything in it and, in a short time, we had caused a huge amount of damage.

We clambered back into the car and screeched off, intending to return to the city centre. Police cars, with their sirens wailing, flew past us in the opposite direction, obviously heading for Bennett's house. This amused us and raised our spirits which, in turn, encouraged us to commit even more attacks. There was a house on the way back, in the Broxholme Lane area, that was an acknowledged meeting place for heroin dealers, so we paid that a visit and gave it the same treatment.

We ended up back in the town centre and, over a glass of lager, we decided to ambush a pub frequented by drug dealers. We checked the area for police and then I told Hazy to lie on the back seat, with the gun pointing out of the window. We circled the pub twice but Hazy lost his bottle.

"This time, you better fucking do it," I threatened him.

I slowed the car to a virtual halt and I yelled at him to start shooting. He indiscriminately blasted the windows of the pub, showering glass everywhere. People were screaming and running out of the pub and we sped off, leaving a scene of pure bedlam.

We dropped Clockwork off at a pub in the market place, while we set off to hide the gun and get changed. When we got back, he had already got the drinks in. We sank pint after pint of Snakebite and smoked several spliffs, against the manager's wishes. Later in the night, much to my surprise, the manager started plying us with free drinks. By the time we left, we were all completely wrecked and elated because of the events earlier in the evening but, when we finally staggered out of the pub, we got the shock of our lives.

We were surrounded by armed policemen, who quickly grabbed me and told me I was under arrest for firearms offences. We were heavily outnumbered, so none of us gave any resistance. We were still on a high and, in a way, this seemed like a fitting end to the night and didn't really bother us. We were cuffed and bundled into a police van, then taken down to the station and locked into the cells for the night.

I woke up the next morning with a nasty hangover and the realisation that I was probably going down for a very long time. Although we had been quite flippant about the arrest the night before, in the sober light of day, I realised the shit I was in. I knew the questioning would soon begin and there was no way I was going to get away with it. Also, I was aware that Hazy was a complete amateur and would probably crack, at the first sign of pressure.

Sure enough, he was quite pathetic, crying and constantly pleading to see me. To his credit, he didn't tell them what they wanted to hear but his hysterics hardly helped our cause. Clockwork was set free because he hadn't really done anything but, as the evidence mounted up, it became increasingly clear that the police had a very strong case against us. I have always felt that when you are obviously going down, the best policy is to play along with the system, as this can take years off your sentence. Villains like to boast about how they told the cops nothing but they are fools, as it gets you nowhere. Eventually, we were put on remand in Doncaster Jail to await trial.

After twelve weeks on remand, we were tried at Doncaster Crown Court. All of mine and Hazy's friends were there and lots of people who had known Sutty were also present. Most people now believed I had nothing to do with Sutty's death, especially after the revenge attack.

The judge, Michael Walker, acknowledged that we were very upset by Sutty's death and could appreciate why we might have wanted revenge but concluded,

"There is nothing more offensive than a sentimental appeal to justice, as an excuse for crime, when it is carried out by confirmed criminals." He recognised that we had been helpful to the police and even told them where the gun was hidden but he still sentenced us both to five years imprisonment after a great deal of plea bargaining.

I recognised that justice did prevail that day, but I was still shocked at the length of the sentence. Hazy fell apart when he heard the verdict and he sobbed as we were taken down to the holding cell, under the court. He was a broken man, unable to cope with the prospect of the sentence he had just been given. For me, it was the most regrettable of all my sentences.

I was thirty-three and I had been out of prison for the longest stretch of my adult life. I had also been in the longest relationship of my life, fathered a child and very nearly made something of myself. Now, the relationship was over, I had lost my baby girl and was facing many long years in jail, for which I no longer felt equipped. Overnight, I had lost everything and I felt very low. We were put into a prison van and, as we drove to Leeds Prison, I reflected on the disaster that was my life. Whatever I did, always seemed to end in trouble and I began to believe that I was doomed from the moment I was born.

Leeds, Full Sutton and Back to Grendon

On arrival in Leeds Prison, I was so depressed that my behaviour was subdued and I lacked any desire to be disruptive. The horrible reality of prison life hit me only too clearly and I wanted nothing to do with it. I vowed to become a model prisoner and go straight when I was eventually released but circumstances meant that such good intentions were to be short-lived.

Not long after I had started my sentence, Bennett, the man who most people felt was responsible for Sutty's death, was admitted to the prison. Quite understandably, he was very pissed off with me because of what had happened to his house and, when we met, there were some very hostile words exchanged. It was obvious that we were going to clash and, although I didn't want any trouble, I couldn't let him get the better of me, or I would become a target for every Tom, Dick and Harry in the jail. When he did confront me, a fight started and I ended up biting off the top of his ear. As punishment, I was moved to the segregation unit in Hull Prison and I lost a substantial amount of remission. When my punishment was over, I was transferred back to Leeds, because the governor of Hull was worried about the amount of influence I had on the other prisoners in his jail.

The welcome I received in Leeds was not warm and, due to various problems, I found myself back in segregation. Although I genuinely wanted to change my ways, I also knew only too well that, in a top security prison, good behaviour is not conducive to survival. Any perceived weakness on my part, would quickly be exploited by my enemies and I had to be prepared to forgo my positive intentions at a moment's notice in order to defend myself.

After two weeks in segregation, I was put back on normal location and given the post of prison barber. This was considered a good job and entailed a great deal of trust on the part of the officers. I repaid their trust by being on my best behaviour and the senior officer was impressed. Unfortunately, some of the local lads were resentful of my position and one, in particular, was very hostile towards me. Because of my efforts to behave and be respectable, he thought he could take liberties with me and was constantly slagging me off and trying to discredit me. When he and his mates started to try and get me sacked from the post, I realised that I couldn't let it go on anymore. I needed to act in a way that would not only deal with him, but also demonstrate to the rest of the prison population that I was not a man to be messed with.

The man in question was called Bob Walters and he was heavily-built and well-respected in the prison. These facts did not deter me from attacking him and I planned to use them to my advantage.

I compiled a list of the informers on my wing and began to tell them that I was under constant psychological attack from Walters. I stressed that these attacks were seriously unsettling and then I alleged that they had extended to physical beatings. Basically, I wanted to convince them that I couldn't take it any longer so that, after I had attacked him, they would tell the screws what terrible provocation I been subjected to. Then, I persuaded one of my mates, Mully, to witness the attack and say that Walters threw the first punch.

Everything was now in place for the assault and, when I felt the time was right, I instructed the informer to wait in the cell and proceeded to fill a large bucket full of boiling water. I hid the bucket by my bed and set off in search of Walters. When I found him, I began to make pathetic excuses for the inconveniences I had caused over the past couple of weeks and asked him to come into my cell, so we could sort things out.

The look of sadistic triumph and arrogance that came over his face enraged me and made me even more determined to give him a lesson he would never forget. Somehow, I managed to conceal my true feelings and suggested a chat over a cup of tea. When he agreed, I had to struggle to suppress a smile. My heart was beating fast but, for my plan to succeed, I had to remain calm.

When we got to my cell, he made himself comfortable on the bed and started to browse through a magazine, as I pretended to make the tea. When his guard was down, I grabbed the bucket of water and poured it all over him. He screamed, but I had anticipated this and had ripped up a towel in preparation, which I now stuffed into his mouth. With that, I began to pound and kick him, concentrating on his face. Bits of flesh fell off, as my fists smashed into him and he clawed at my neck and face, in a desperate attempt to stop me. As he fell to the floor, I pulled out my blade and began to jump up and down on his body, stabbing him about the head and face.

Mully could not believe this display of gross violence and it was only the look of abject horror on his face that prevented me from killing Walters. Mully was a gypsy and was well known in the criminal fraternity as a very hard man, who was difficult to shock. So, when I saw his reaction, it brought me to my senses.

Before the screws arrived, I removed the gag, to make it look less like a completely premeditated attack. From their assessment of the situation, it was obvious who was the loser but, because of the slight injuries I had suffered, it was impossible to say who had started it.

This incident was so serious that I was interviewed by the Leeds police but, because I stuck rigidly to my story and was backed up by Mully, they had little choice but to recommend that the matter should be dealt with internally. Despite the fact that it was the worst assault in the prison for fifteen years, it was whitewashed over and, after sixty days in solitary, I was transferred to Full Sutton, a new, top security prison.

On arrival at Full Sutton, I was put straight into the segregation unit because of the assault at Leeds. My reputation had preceded me and the screws were ready to jump on me at every opportunity. Anything that happened in the prison was immediately blamed on me and it was a very uncomfortable time. This vendetta against me, by the prison establishment, came to a head with a terrifying incident, as a result of which they then tried to incarcerate me in a secure mental hospital.

I accepted that I had done some crazy things and continued to suffer from psychological problems but there was no way I was mad. However, the staff at Full Sutton were convinced that I should be sent to a prison for the criminally insane, such as Broadmoor or Parkhurst and, as a first step, I was sent to Grendon Underwood for psychiatric analysis. In reality, it was obvious that I was not insane but if they decided I was, there would be no second opinion, I would simply never be seen, or heard of, again.

Thankfully, the staff at Grendon, who had previously worked so hard to help me, were not going to play along with what I believe was a plan to get rid of me for good and they declared that psychiatric treatment was unnecessary. I was hastily returned to Full Sutton and put back into segregation.

The thought of how close I had come to being locked away forever, shook me to the core. This was the first time that the establishment had used underhand methods against me and it was very harrowing to face the stark truth, that my life was completely in their hands. I suppose it had been the case for most of the last thirty odd years but now it struck me hard that my status as a person, my individuality, was gone. I was just a number in a system.

This incident precipitated a long period of depression, which was aggravated by the physical surroundings of the the prison. Its low ceilings seemed to bear down on me, adding to my feelings of oppression, restriction and claustrophobia. Also, the prison, which was still in its infancy, was experiencing many teething problems.

The regime was constantly changing and the communication between different sections of the prison was abysmal. This meant procedures were often carried out incorrectly and, basically, it seemed as if nobody had proper, over-all control of the running of the place. In this very unstable environment, my mental well-being dwindled to the point where I was on the verge of a breakdown.

There was also a constant barrage of police interviews, concerning previous crimes, to contend with and they would always leave me feeling stressed and exhausted. After one such interview, I was trying to relax in my cell, when a note was pushed under the door. The contents informed me that Elaine, who had always stuck so faithfully by me, had died of cancer.

Although I had never been in love with her, this news devastated me. She had been a truly caring person and her loyalty had inspired me to try to go straight on my release and form an honest life with her. Perhaps this was a lofty ambition that I could never have fulfilled, but Elaine represented a degree of hope to me and now she was gone, I was left in a lonely, emotional vacuum.

My failures, both in my personal and criminal life, along with my traumatic relationship with Jacky, haunted me. I felt totally numb and became vacant and withdrawn. The only thing I had to look forward to was getting off the segregation unit and I vowed to deal with my problems and start normal location on a positive note. I nearly managed to accomplish this aim when I was again struck by a piece of bad news. A child I had fathered in a previous relationship had been killed in a road accident.

Although I had had little to do with my daughter, I was shattered. There seemed to be nothing left for me. Because of prison bureaucracy, I was not even allowed to attend either of the funerals and my deep depression and frustration manifested itself, once again, in disruptive behaviour. My frequent temper tantrums resulted in me smashing up prison furniture and acting aggressively towards the staff. I constantly engaged in subversion; pressing alarm bells, arson, sit-downs and, inevitably, became heavily-involved with the prison's sub-culture.

None of these things was of any value to my future, either inside or outside prison, but I had lost all interest in my life and was on a downward slide. Fortunately, some of the staff were perceptive enough to detect this in me and I was given the job of wing cleaner, a position which involved a great degree of trust. They realised that to punish me would be pointless. I had already had enough of that and there was nothing they could do that would bother me anymore. By giving me the job, they gave me something to be proud of. It also gave me a certain amount of autonomy, which made me feel more like a person again and less resentful of the prison officers. I now had something to live for and, although it was only small, it gave me the necessary degree of self-respect to look to the future and to change myself.

This move by the prison staff paid immediate dividends, with an immediate improvement in both my attitude and behaviour. I gave up all forms of subversion but, if I felt that something was not right, I would not hesitate in speaking up. Instead of voicing my problems through violence, I used my brain and, although I was not regarded as an easy prisoner by staff or inmates, I slowly began to gain their respect.

I saw it as a personal challenge to seek out injustice in the prison and some of the changes I influenced marked me out as a very strong member of the community on D Wing. Such positive behaviour was essential at this stage of socialisation in Full Sutton, which had only been open for eighteen months and the officers acknowledged this, by giving me little perks. I used such respect from the staff to cultivate positive thinking amongst my peer group which, in turn, helped develop good relations between staff and inmates.

The end result was that I was rewarded with two home leaves, which were undertaken without any problems. They gave me the chance, not only to visit the graves of Elaine and my daughter, but also their relatives. When I had accomplished this, I felt that a great weight had been lifted from me. I hadn't realised just how deeply these deaths had affected me. I hadn't been allowed to attend their funerals and these leaves gave me the chance to put them to rest in my mind.

The responsibility I had shown in taking my leaves without incident, along with the exemplary way I had carried out my cleaning duties, did not go unnoticed and most of the remission I had lost, due to the assault at Leeds and various incidents in Full Sutton, was restored. This was concrete recognition of my efforts to change my ways and I felt very good about it. It convinced me that, under this regime, good behaviour would be rewarded, a concept that did not exist in the conventional prisons I had experienced previously.

During one of the home leaves, I met a woman called Tina Jefferies, daughter of Alex Jeffries, Doncaster's famous footballer, with six England caps to his name. We had known each other for ten years and, although I had always been attracted to her, I had never considered approaching her, as she was not criminally-inclined. She was a very decent, respectable girl and, with my past, I thought it would have been unrealistic to try and get involved with her. However, my confidence was buoyed by my changed attitude and behaviour and the progress I was making, so I mustered up enough courage to ask her to accompany me on an evening out.

Without hesitation, she turned me down flatly, making it completely clear that she wanted nothing to do with someone with my reputation. I wasn't particularly surprised but continued to badger her throughout the remainder of my week's home leave, until she eventually consented to a quiet evening in a country pub, on my last evening.

I think Tina was taken aback when she found that I actually came across as a far more intelligent and sensitive person than the image I had portrayed in and around the town centre. The evening was very pleasant and, despite feeling that it would lead to nothing, I asked Tina to write to me in prison. She agreed to write on a 'no strings attached' basis and her letters, though timid at first, were very comforting, especially in the light of Elaine's death.

I was beginning to feel I had a future outside prison and, when Tina began to visit me in Full Sutton, I was overjoyed. The possibility that we would get together now seemed very likely and I was desperate to prove to her that I was a changed man and worthy of her consideration. Tina might be prepared to forgive my past behaviour but the rest of the population of Doncaster was not so understanding and we both recognised the importance of keeping our involvement secret.

Eventually, Tina's father was made aware of our relationship by the police, who felt it was their moral duty to warn him to keep his daughter away from me. They must have been informed about the relationship by the prison officers and this conspiratorial attitude disheartened me. The last few months had helped me forge positive links with the prison staff and I thought the 'us and them' situation was improving in the jail. This event demonstrated to me that I was still regarded as a loser by the prison staff and it destroyed my faith in them. Nevertheless, I was determined to continue behaving well and secure my freedom as soon as possible.

On my eventual release in 1989, I moved into Tina's house in a nice suburb of Doncaster called Bessacarr. Most people were completely opposed to any sort of relationship between us, so there was uproar when I moved in. I suppose it did seem premature, but it was really a practical arrangement, as I had nowhere else to stay and no cash whatsoever. If the relationship had failed, I would have left immediately but we were both confident enough about our future together, for me to move in.

Only a few months ago I had nothing but, here I was, sharing a beautiful house, with a woman who I really cared for and her lovely daughter. At first, I felt nothing but happiness but soon this turned to frustration, when I was unable to get a job and provide for them. I felt totally worthless. All I could claim to own was a bad reputation and a despicable criminal record. Nobody wanted to employ an ex-con, especially when unemployment figures were so high already.

Over the next six weeks, I applied for hundreds of jobs, but nobody would take me on. All the progress in Full Sutton had come to nothing. It seemed like the establishment encouraged you to go straight while you were in prison but when you were released, you were on your own. This state of affairs is surely ridiculous if the intention is to reduce the level of crime in the country.

To add to my despondency, I was also being constantly harassed by the police. They followed me wherever I went, asking me stupid questions and repeatedly searching me. In one thirty-six hour period, I received four parking tickets for no reason but, worst of all, I was arrested and questioned about a murder I could not possibly have committed.

The police hauled me in and charged me with murdering a woman who had been killed while I was locked up in Full Sutton. They said that they had found traces of blood in the boot of my car and that was why I had been arrested. I told them that it was not surprising that there was blood in my car, as I had bought it from a livestock farmer, only two days ago and, sure enough, the traces turned out to be pigs' blood. I might have done some crazy things in my time but the suggestion that I could have killed a woman insulted me. The police obviously knew that I wasn't responsible and were just trying to wind me up.

While all this was going on, I also became aware of how popular I had become. My fearsome reputation, exaggerated by the constant police harassment, seemed to make me some kind of folk hero in certain sections of the community. This was very confusing as here I was trying to forge a new life for myself, whilst some people still idolised the man I used to be. I found their attentions very counter-productive, as they kept my past misdemeanours fresh in the minds of my critics, who still thought I was a villain.

These were the main reasons why I began to suffer from what is termed post-release stress. My paranoia returned and I began to suffer from anxiety attacks, which were usually accompanied by bouts of hyper-mania. My frustrations became exaggerated and I found it difficult to interact socially. Basically, I was a wreck and I needed help but, apart from Tina, there was nobody I could turn to. The state didn't want to know and the only contact I had with it was the constant, unhelpful attention from the police.

Although I don't cite these things as an excuse for my resumption of criminal activities, they are certainly the reasons and I think they explain it, to a great extent. My attitude to crime had completely changed and it was with conscious regret that I once again resorted to illegal methods to get money. When the police detest you and you are an outcast from normal society, the moral questions surrounding criminality are removed. I wasn't going to use violence unless I really had to and, then, only against other criminals. Breaking the law meant nothing to me, as I knew that the law could be as crooked as any criminal.

When Doncaster's criminal fraternity realised I was back in circulation, I was inundated with offers of 'a piece of the action'. I was merely interested in making money and mostly acted as a fence for stolen goods. I had never felt any guilt or remorse about my previous crimes, they were simply not sentiments that a dedicated criminal was capable of feeling. The threat of incarceration had been regarded as an occupational hazard and the prize had always seemed worth the risk of a jail sentence. Now, I participated half-heartedly, depressingly resigned to the fact that my activities would probably land me back in prison. This feeling of inevitability was quite powerful and, though I definitely didn't want to go back inside, I figured I was bound to, eventually, whatever I did. I considered the need to make money, to support Tina and her daughter, as paramount, so any dreams of an honest life were doomed.

I stumbled along for a while, engaging in various crimes and it felt good to be earning again. I still felt I would probably be in prison before long and, although I kept a fairly low profile, it was not long before I found myself confronted by a big problem.

Bob and the Cigarettes

It all started when I went to meet a guy called Bob, who regularly bought stolen goods from me. I had supplied him with three thousand pound's worth of cigarettes and tobacco that I had received and he had agreed to pay me one-thousand, six-hundred pounds for them. We always settled payment in a pub and we had decided to meet at Sunday lunchtime and have a few drinks in the Rising Sun, in the town centre. I was accompanied by my brother Vincent and, when we arrived, we found Bob in the company of a group of blokes we both knew. Our suspicions were immediately aroused, as they were acting strangely and were quite verbally aggressive towards us. They were normally quiet, reserved guys and it was obvious that something was amiss.

After a few hours drinking, the cigarettes had still not been mentioned and I was becoming very agitated. Eventually, I asked him directly about the money and he let out a stream of abuse that did not go unnoticed by the other customers in the pub. When he finally calmed down, it turned out that he was pissed off because the consignment had been short, to the tune of seventy-two pound's worth of pipe tobacco. I accepted his allegation, without fuss and was relieved to find out that this was all that was bothering him. After quickly suggesting that he should only give me one and a half grand and reassuring him that I would personally cover the outstanding tobacco, we agreed to meet that evening in the same pub but I left feeling unsettled.

Bob and his associates had been very hostile and had issued some serious threats. He was a well-known member of the criminal fraternity, with a string of convictions and I knew he was capable of carrying out his threats but it all seemed a little extreme, considering only seventy-two quid's worth of goods was missing. I could see no real reason for his attitude and I was apprehensive about our meeting later that evening.

I went home to Bessacarr, showered, ate my Sunday lunch and slept for three hours. Tina woke me early in the evening and I had another shower to freshen up and then retrieved my gun and ammunition and concealed them in my car. Tina was working in her father's pub that night, so I suggested she come along with Vinnie and me, for a drink in the pub where I was going to meet Bob. She wasn't fully aware of what I was up to and neither she, nor Vinnie, knew I had my gun.

On the way into town, we picked up Vinny and then carried on to the pub. Bob and I had arranged to do business in the car park, as I anticipated some trouble from him and didn't want it to spill into the pub, where Tina and my brother would be drinking. The car park was deserted, he was nowhere to be seen but I kept calm and we all went inside for a drink.

The pub was strangely empty and there was no sign of Bob or his associates. The landlady said she had not seen him all night and that he had certainly not left an envelope with money in it for me. Clearly, Bob was playing games and me and Vinny quickly decided that one of us should go to his house, which was only about one hundred yards from the pub. Tina had been chatting to someone and wasn't aware of what was going on, so we told her that I was just nipping out to the car, as I still didn't expect him to be much of a problem.

I drove round and jumped out of the car. The hall and lounge light were on, so I walked up to the door, which was made of glass, and knocked. I didn't want any trouble and hoped he would just come out and hand over the cash. Net curtains obscured my view but, since the lights were on, I assumed he must be in there. When nobody answered, I banged a little louder and, when there was still no answer, I jumped back in the car and drove round for a few minutes, agitated, planning my next move.

I was still convinced that he was at home and just deliberately not answering, which annoyed me, so I drove back and sounded my horn a few times. There was still no response, so I marched up to the door and started banging on it very noisily. This brought a few of his neighbours out of their houses, to see what all the commotion was about.

By this time, I was extremely pissed off. Bob had no cause to ignore me and, as I had offered to more than repay the missing tobacco, I could only assume he was deliberately trying to avoid payment. Although I kept outwardly calm, I was inwardly seething and, if I had seen him then, I would have done him serious damage. He couldn't be allowed to get away with it, or every crook in Doncaster would start taking liberties with me.

I retrieved my gun from the car and blasted a hole through his front door, in the hope that this would bring him to his senses. I jumped back into the car and drove calmly round to the pub, to rejoin Tina and my brother. After drinking half a lager with them, it was time for Tina to go to work and, as I drove to her father's pub, I noticed a heavy police presence in the city centre. This didn't concern me, as they had been harassing me since I got out of prison and I was used to the sight of them.

After dropping Tina off, I returned to the Rising Sun. There were a large number of officers there and it was soon apparent that they were looking for me. I got out of the car and started to hurl abuse at them, telling them to leave me alone. Apparently, Bob's neighbours were concerned by all the noise and had taken my registration number and called the police. They didn't mention the gun, so I shouted some more abuse at them and then strode into the pub and ordered a drink.

The gun was under the back seat of my car, so I knew I would be found out in the end but there was no way I was going to give myself up to the bastards, who would be congratulating themselves, now that they had got me again. I sat in the pub, downing another lager, when the police, complete with reinforcements, burst in and arrested me. I didn't offer them any resistance but they still manhandled me, as they put on the handcuffs and hauled me down to the station. In my frustration, I was calling them every name under the sun but they weren't bothered, just smug that they had caught me again.

Obviously I was disappointed, as the prospect of another prison sentence loomed but it did not come as a surprise. At this point in my life, I simply accepted that it was my fate and that I was doomed to spend most of my life in prison. I didn't whinge about it, or use it as an excuse for my behaviour, I simply felt that whatever I did, always resulted with me back inside. This time, I had lost a woman who loved me, a family and a home and this hurt but, again, I still doubted that it would ever have worked, as they were normal people and, frankly, I wasn't. Even so, it did come as a massive shock when I was sentenced to a seven year extended sentence with a recommendation that I serve every day of it.

The type of firearms offence I had committed would normally carry a maximum sentence of three years but I had previous convictions, which I had calculated would go against me. I prepared myself for a sentence of up to five years, hoping I would be able to get out in about three, so I was astounded when the judge, David Bentley, pronounced sentence. According to him, the main reason for the length of the sentence was a report, submitted to the court by the probation service. This report was riddled with ambiguity and concluded that I was a dangerously psychotic man. How they could assume this, without any psychological assessment, was not explained and I can only conclude that it was written in an attempt to keep me inside for as long as possible.

I was sent down and then rapidly transferred to Hull prison. This was only a temporary measure and, within eighteen hours, I was transferred to Full Sutton. I arrived there in the morning but wasn't allowed to leave the reception area, as the governors were having a meeting to decide which wing I should be placed on. It transpired that nobody wanted me on their wing. In fact, they didn't want me in the prison at all and it looked like I was in for another transfer, until the number one governor, Barry Smith, intervened.

I was directed to D Wing, where I had been housed during my last stay at Full Sutton and immediately the reception ritual began. I had been through this process on so many occasions that it was nothing more than a dull, all-too- familiar routine. In an effort to get it over quickly, I told the various welfare officers, psychologists and governors whatever they wanted to hear.

After the reception process, came my introduction to the wing governor, who confirmed that I was going to serve the full term of my sentence, without parole and that any further acts of violence would result in my sentence being extended to life. This was a terrifying prospect. I was in a top security prison, alongside some of Britain's most violent men and understood, only too clearly, that conflict was a part of everyday life. Avoiding trouble in no way guaranteed that I would not have to fight to defend myself. Of course, the screws knew this and were well aware of the vulnerability of my position but they relished it, as they could now call all the shots.

It was apparent that the authorities had finally had enough of me and were going to try and keep me locked up forever. My fatalistic prophecy was coming true and I was about to spend the rest of my years in jail. I was filled with dread but, most of all, I felt extreme hatred for members of the establishment and I determined to be as disruptive as possible.

In the following weeks, I pressed alarm bells, smashed workshops and generally involved myself in any riotous activity going on in the jail. I made preparations to escape but then decided on a much more bloody way to leave prison.

I was going to take a member of staff hostage and then severely wound, if not kill him. I wanted to take out a governor but, if that wasn't possible, a screw would have to do. Afterwards, I planned on mustering enough courage to take my own life. I couldn't face the prospect of spending years in prison and, if the only way to leave was in a box, then so be it.

Fortunately, I didn't get the chance to put my plan into action and, out of frustration, I smashed up a workshop and climbed onto the roof. I screamed insults about the staff, inmates and prison management and, when I finally came down, I was thrown straight into segregation. While I rotted in segregation, my mind filled with murderous thoughts, it was decided that I should be sent to the new, million pound Special Unit, in Hull Prison.

The rest of my stay at Full Sutton was spent in permanent segregation, along with some of the most dangerous men in the British penal system. They had all committed horrendous crimes and, in society's eyes, they were not fit to walk the earth. To me, they were just fellow inmates and they were the only human beings with whom I could have a proper converstation. Some were crazy, some just plain bad; I took them as I found them and some became very good friends.

Andrzy 'Jacko' Jakubczyk was serving fifteen years for armed robbery and hostage-taking and was known by the media as the 'Million Pound Prisoner'. He earned this name because of the huge amount of costly disruption and damage he caused. He was such a difficult case that he was constantly being shifted from prison to prison, at a cost to the public of three thousand pounds per transfer.

Jacko was a very unpredictable and complex man but he was also highly intelligent and had a sensitive side. He felt he was fighting a one man war against the system and he was very devious and determined. We often talked for hours and I have a lot to thank him for. He showed me that violence was not the best way to hurt people or stand up for myself. He explained the power of words to me and told me that the pen, not the gun, must become my tool. Jacko also taught me that the best way to deal with the sadistic mind games that some screws liked to play was not to react violently, but to reverse roles and play them at their own game. I observed how he dealt with the screws and soon found that, I too, could manipulate them, if I used my brain.

Another prisoner in the 'seg', at the same time as me was Dennis Nielson, the infamous serial killer, who was responsible for killing and mutilating sixteen young men. Such a high-profile prisoner was obviously the subject of much discussion amongst the inmates and many were fearful of him. I didn't share this fear and was intrigued by the man. Curious to meet him, one day, when I knew he was exercising, I demanded that I be allowed to talk to him.

The guards were reluctant to let me into the exercise cage and were suspicious of my motives. Eventually, they realised that I wasn't going to take no for an answer and opened the cage. Dennis looked bemused as I bounced confidently into the cage but, he kept his cool, and nodded to acknowledge me. We soon got chatting and, contrary to what I had been told about him and the horrific nature of his crimes, he came across as a very pleasant and humorous man.

Back in segregation, we would often talk and I found him to be an excellent conversationalist. He was intelligent and very well read and was philosophical about the prospect of his life sentence.

Other men on the segregation wing were more volatile. One of these was Ricky Peterson, who received a seven year sentence for kidnapping and robbery but was now certified insane and likely to spend the rest of his years in jail. He was a huge man, who spent most of his time lifting weights. He was extremely dangerous and was so strong that he was shackled whenever he was out of his cell.

Tragically, he had completely lost his mind whilst in prison and had changed his name to Charles Bronson, as he was obsessed with the star of the 'Death Wish' movies. The psychotic delusions he frequently suffered from caused him to flip and damage anything or anybody within reach. At first, we were friends but he has since vowed to kill me at the first given opportunity. I do not doubt that Bronson would carry out his threat but I still retain some sympathy for a man tortured by a terrible mental illness.

The 'seg' also housed a record-breaker in Dougie Wakefield. Dougie was serving life, with a recommendation of at least twenty-five years inside, for two murders. One of these killings was committed in prison and he had also tried to kill prison officers on various occasions. He was in the Guinness Book of Records as the man to have spent the longest time in solitary confinement in any British prison.

Living with such a motley crew certainly made life in segregation interesting, if not a little hectic and the night before my transfer was no exception. Tired but restless, I was lying on my bed with my mind in overdrive. From the next cell, I could hear Jacko calling for the guards to come and let him out, as he claimed he was ill. I knew he was planning something, so I sat up to listen to the drama which was bound to follow.

There were only two guards present during the night and there had to be six there to open a cell, so four screws had to return to the prison before Jacko could be let out. This was the sort of inconvenience that he loved to create and it was great to watch the screws getting pissed off with him, knowing that they had to let him out.

When they finally opened the door, he immediately attacked them, which resulted in him getting severely beaten and then thrown back into his cell. As soon as the screws had turned round, he cut his wrists and demanded the attention of a doctor. A doctor had to be brought from the nearby York Hospital, as the prison doctor had gone home. The poor man had never had to deal with a situation like this and you could tell from his voice that he was terrified.

Jacko behaved like the perfect gentleman and thanked the doctor profusely for his help. He told him that he had slit his wrists after becoming depressed and, when he asked for help, the prison staff had beaten him. We joined in the disruption, by banging our cell doors and slagging off the screws at the top of our voices. This kept the rest of the prison awake and, in turn, their clamour added to the electrifying atmosphere.

Suddenly, my cell door swung open and in stepped four screws from Hull prison. I recognised one of them, as having been involved in the beating of one of my pals, Paul Hill, one of the Birmingham Six. The other screws who had carried out the beating had all been prosecuted but this one had got away with it and he was hated by all the prisoners who knew him. They ordered me to pack my kit, which I did as quickly as possible, then marched out of the cell, pushing past the screws.

I walked past all the cell doors, so I could say my goodbyes and all the inmates wished me luck and told me to keep my head up. Jacko was slumped in his cell, looking terrible, after the beating he'd just taken.

"I'm going to kill myself, Frankie," he told me in a calm voice. I looked down at him and then shouted defiantly, at the top of my voice,

"If you have to die, then make sure you kill the screws first!"

The officers from Hull grabbed me and handcuffed me. I stode off along the wing as quickly as possible, with the screws almost jogging to keep up. All around me, the prisoners were screaming abuse at the staff and I revelled in the mayhem although, curiously, I was sad to be leaving.

They locked me into the van and I was whisked straight to Hull, with not a word spoken by me or the officers. As soon as we got to Hull, I was taken straight to the Special Unit: a prison within a prison.

The Special Unit

The Special Unit was one of three, top security units in the country, set up to house those inmates who were considered too dangerous and disruptive for the normal prison system. The unit aimed to provide humane treatment of prisoners in a relaxed atmosphere, with a massive emphasis placed on education, in the hope that this would help the inmates to address their offending behaviour and, perhaps, strive to change. The most radical feature of the unit was that, unlike other prisons, the stress was on rehabilitation rather than punishment.

The first unit of this kind was set up in the Seventies at Barlinnie Prison in Glasgow and its initial development was famously documented in the book 'A Sense of Freedom', by Jimmy Boyle. However, there are still only a handful of them in Britain and they are in jeopardy because they are very unpopular with the conservative and right-wing Prison Officers Association. I now consider them to be the most progressive and effective way for dealing with the offending behaviour of serious criminals but, when I arrived there in 1989, I didn't believe that anything to do with the prison service could benefit me in the slightest.

The first thing that struck me about the unit was its size. I later came to know it as the 'concrete submarine,' which is a pretty apt description. There were screws everywhere, four to every one of the ten inmates, and this really irritated me. I was shown to my cell and left to unpack and settle in.

In a new jail, it is never a good idea to go round introducing yourself to the other inmates. Some will take it the wrong way and the last thing you want to do in a high security prison is make enemies on your first day. The first person to come and introduce himself was a bloke called Micky Holliday. He started telling me how he was 'the chap of the gaff' and how everybody respected him. I can smell bullshit from a mile off and it was obvious that Micky was talking bollocks but I didn't want to cause any trouble, so I just let him ramble on, until he eventually left. I found out that his nickname was Walter Mitty, because of these tall tales.

Some time later, a heavily-tattooed young Scot walked into my cell, whose face seemed familiar. He introduced himself as 'the famous Kevin O'Neil' but said that everyone called him 'Kevo'. He was serving a life sentence, with a recommendation to serve forty-five years.

It was then that I recognised him as the psychopath who had stalked the streets of London, torturing and murdering vagrants and down and outs. He was a psychopath in the true sense of the word and was infamous rather than famous. I told him that I had heard about him and he simply said,

"Hey, it is I, Kevo, doomed for life but, through my art, I'm free."

I didn't know what the fuck he was talking about but he seemed friendly enough, so I smiled and told him I'd see him later.

Immediately after Kevo's departure, in wobbled another Jock, Fat Fred Low, who I knew from my time in Wakefield, in the early eighties, where we had both witnessed the horrific murder of two inmates by a fellow prisoner, Robert Mosely. Low had now followed in Mosely's footsteps and killed a harmless inmate in Gartree prison, simply to gain notoriety. He had only been on a relatively short sentence for assaulting and robbing pensioners but now he was in for natural life. He introduced himself briefly and then, thankfully, left me to my own devices.

I could hear him prattling on to the other inmates about how "me and Frank go back a long way" and I began to despair. How was I going to endure seven years of being locked in a special unit with this shower of crap? Most of them were fucking lunatics and, as if that wasn't bad enough, there were screws breathing down your neck every minute of the day. Not just regular screws either; these were handpicked for their ability to talk to difficult inmates but, even more importantly, being able to fight and control them, if necessary.

The last prisoner to make his approach on that first day was Alan 'Queenie' McGraw. After telling me his name, he announced that he was a queer and that he wanted me to hear it from him and not the other inmates who, he said, all slagged him off behind his back. Later, I discovered that, even though this was the case, when they felt a little horny, they would quite happily sneak down to his cell and let him suck their pricks. I didn't have a problem with queers anymore, after all, it was a central part of prison life but I'm fucked if I'd let a bloke suck my knob, no matter how desperate I got.

My next visitor was an officer and I was actually glad to have the company of a normal person. He was called Tony Clark and was one of the four personal officers assigned specifically to me.

"I know you hate screws, Frank," he told me, "but if you need to talk, or some advice, you can always come to me."

"Cheers, but I don't think I'll be needing you," I replied. The mind games on the unit had started.

Over the next few hours, I looked around my new surroundings and was surprised at the amount of movement the prisoners were allowed. This was slightly disconcerting at first, as I was used to having a screw watch over me, wherever I went. The facilities were the best I had ever come across but the large number of staff present at all times was really starting to eat into me. I still harboured a great hatred for the 'system' and it didn't take long before a screw was on the receiving end of my explosive temper.

Everything had gone pretty smoothly for the first few weeks and, although the unit hadn't had any curative effect on me, I certainly hadn't caused any trouble. But, late one night, I stumbled across the principal officer, a man we called Tate and nicknamed 'Spudhead', trying to manipulate a black lad, Everton, about a racial issue. He was winding the lad up, which was bang out of order and I just snapped.

I grabbed a pool cue and broke it over his head. He staggered back against the wall and I pinned him there, holding the broken piece up to his face. Everton looked on, his eyes virtually popping out of his head in excitement. He had picked up a lump of glass, ready to jump in, if the situation kicked off. I could literally feel the blood pumping through my veins and I raised the splintered end of the cue, up to Spudhead's eye. All the other inmates had been awakened by now and were tooled up and eagerly awaiting my next move.

All my hatred of screws was focused on Spudhead Tate's petrified, contorted face, making me want to fire the end of the cue right through his eye socket but I had retained just enough self-control to realise that, with all the inmates ready to kick off, if I succumbed to the urge, there would be a blood bath. Suddenly, another officer, Ron Cooper, ambled onto the unit, seemingly oblivious to the seriousness of the situation.

"Nay, Frankie, come on, this is not what you're all about," he urged, in his thick, Humberside accent. Spudhead was pouring with sweat and his lips trembled, as he mouthed a silent prayer. I brought the cue closer to his eye, but kept my gaze fixed on Ron.

"Nay, nay, Frankie. Calm down, lad," he said softly. I looked into his eyes and I could read nothing but true concern, compassion and honesty. Instantly, my anger evaporated and I felt very silly and exposed. In the past, my reaction to such an uncomfortable situation would have automatically been violence but, uncharacteristically, I kept my cool. The pool cue slid from my hand and I walked quietly back to my cell.

I was flooded with a sea of confusing emotions, which left my mind reeling. I wanted to cry but I couldn't. With my brain in turmoil, I sat there anticipating a beating by the screws, followed by a sedative injection but it didn't happen. Surely I would be thrown into solitary for attacking an officer?

In the event, no punishment was given at all, as the Special Unit did not use any punitive measures. This left me to contemplate my actions, which was far more painful than a stint in solitary, where the humiliation of being caged-in, quickly turned to anger and left no room for remorse. The unit quietened down over the next few weeks and my only real contact with the screws was them popping into my cell, to check how I was.

Ron Cooper, whom we had dubbed 'Ron the Red', because of his socialist views, was the most helpful and my favourite among the staff. He was constantly lending me books, assuring me that I was a bright lad and should be trying to educate myself. He told me that I could achieve university standard if I really tried and that I had the ability to change. At first, I dismissed what he was saying as bollocks but, gradually, his persistence began to pay off.

One day, I was bored out of my skull and I wandered into the art and craft studio, where our artist in residence, Steve Dove, was clearing up. He said hello and I nodded in acknowledgement. He rattled on, talking about the art and craft room and asking me question after question. I still wasn't comfortable with the staff and mistrusted them all, so I remained tight-lipped, only replying to his incessant questions with the odd grunt. Unconsciously, I had picked up a lump of loose clay and, throughout the conversation, had been shaping it with my hands.

"Did you do that?" asked Dovey, pointing to the clay in my hands. I looked down and realised that I had moulded the clay into the figure of a man lying down. I nodded, feeling slightly embarrassed.

"You're a fucking sculptor, lad," laughed Dovey. I grinned slightly and walked awkwardly back out to my cell, locking the door behind me.

As I lay on my bed, the clay figure started to really bother me. I felt like I'd let my defences down: the figure was a part of me, on display for everyone to see. I had to destroy it. I jumped up, sprinted down the stairs and burst into the classroom. To my surprise, Dovey, Red Ron and a governor called Peter Bennett, were standing around my figure, deep in discussion.

"Here he is, the sculptor," smiled Ron.

"I can't," I blurted out, but Dovey just took the figure and locked it in the kiln, so that I was unable to retrieve it.

Unnerved, I walked out of the classroom, leaving the other two chatting away. Ron sensed how much it was bothering me and he urged me to chill out.

"Go and play with some clay, Frankie lad," he suggested. I didn't want to hurt Ron's feelings but I really didn't want to start messing about with clay. I was scared that people would laugh at me, that I would become weak.

"I'm a villain, not a normal bloke, Ron. I can't do it," I explained to him.

"Nonsense, Frank, you're as good as the next man, son. Give yourself a break. Besides, I thought you gypos were supposed to have bottle." He'd done his homework and knew I was from a gypsy background. I took this as a sign that he really was concerned about me.

"We'll see," I said and scurried back to my cell.

That night, my mind was filled with confusion about who I was and what I wanted to be. I was starting to yearn for something different – a complete change of direction. The hate and venom I felt for the system was holding me back, restricting new possibilities, as it took up all my energy and, the end result, was always nothing. Besides, it was hard to sustain my hatred of the screws when they included people like Ron, who was undeniably trying to help me. I wanted to direct my energies into something more positive and, I thought, pottery might just be the starting point, if not the solution.

Because of my strong personality, the other lads on the unit had started to identify me as their leader. Whilst this gave me a privileged position amongst them, it also meant they would all come to me with their problems. I was acting like a social worker, counselling them on anything from drugs to wanking. But everything they talked about was negative. In the past, I had loved talking about violence, subversion and crime but now it burdened me down. Strangely, all I could think about was my clay model.

The next day, I went down to the classroom and demanded aggressively that the door be opened. The screw looked uncomfortable but, after the nod from a cordial colleague, he hesitantly opened the door. I stormed into the room and plunged my hands into a vat of terracotta clay. I pulled out a big lump and began to manipulate it roughly. The sensation of the clay in my hands was incredible and, although it was a new experience for me, deep down it felt familiar. I worked at a ferocious pace, churning out piece after piece.

This frantic creativity continued over the next few weeks and Ron the Red and Steve Dove, constantly offered me support and encouragement. They took my work very seriously and we often had lengthy discussions during which, they treated me as an intellectual equal. From time to time, a top local sculptress came to visit and it was very interesting to talk to her about my newly- discovered talent. All the attention was certainly flattering but I was also embarrassed. I had plunged into this new world and I was simultaneously puzzled and intrigued by it. I still had reservations and worries but I had an even stronger feeling that this was something more important than I had ever done and this conviction spurred me on.

The other lads on the unit had also started to take up various hobbies and I tried to encourage them and help them whenever I could. Kevo had revealed himself to be an excellent painter and was adept with pastels. His pictures were always of clowns and I was very impressed by them. The unit was buzzing and I really felt that progress was being made. There were still problems: at least one inmate a day would have a little tantrum but, on the whole, the atmosphere was very constructive.

The governor was also impressed. Here were the scum of the country, knuckling under and getting on with their bird. Unfortunately, some of the screws did not share his optimism. They were used to treating us like shit and we responded by acting like animals which, in their minds, justified their behaviour. When we actually began to achieve something, they were unable to accept that inmates could accomplish anything worthwhile. The vicious circle of violence which perpetuated their views was being broken and they resented it.

The tools, paintbrushes and materials, mysteriously began to vanish and it always happened when we were locked up. It was obvious that it was deliberate sabotage on the part of the screws. Tension rose but, luckily, in Peter Bennet, we had an excellent governor, who was always able to diffuse potentially explosive situations.

The work being produced in the Special Unit was of such a high standard, that it was decided that it should be exhibited. An internal exhibition was arranged and various local dignitaries were invited. This was quite an unusual occurrence in a prison and the Home Office was worried that we would take advantage of the situation. They were especially worried that there could be hostage-taking. However, we repaid our debt of trust and behaved impeccably.

Amongst the guests were Brian Leuchford, head of security for the Home Office and the Mayor of Hull. Various clergymen turned up and there were people from the local and national media to report on the event. I took particular care to acquaint myself with some of the journalists, so that I could use them to make my voice heard on the outside.

The highlight of the afternoon was when Louise Carson, head of fine arts at the Ferrins Art Gallery in Hull, announced that the gallery wished to buy my 'Prehistoric Fish' for seven hundred pounds. This was the best news I had heard in years. The media were allowed to interview me and Kevo and I told them that I was committed to becoming an artist, so that I would have a platform from which to speak out about the situation in Britain's prisons and about crime on the streets.

The success of the exhibition proved to me that I should build on the progress I had made. The fears and doubts I had harboured about sculpting were washed away and I was determined to succeed and take my message to as many people as possible. Finally, I perceived an opportunity to reveal what prison was really like but I knew had to tread cautiously. I had to be careful not to antagonise the authorities too much as, ultimately, it was they who controlled my destiny.

I realised that simply sculpting was not enough. I had to raise my media profile and this meant expanding into other areas and, perhaps, exaggerating the truth a little, along the way. Things had been going fairly quietly, so I contacted the national and local media and told them that my work had been accepted and acclaimed in America. This was utter bullshit but who was to prove me wrong? As a result, interest in me vastly increased and I was regularly in the papers and on television. The North of England now knew me as Frank Cook, the artist and prison reformer and not South Yorkshire's most dangerous gunman.

My new-found status made some of the staff feel uncomfortable. They realised that I was just as belligerent as ever but now I had exchanged the gun for the pen and my violence was verbal. My behaviour was stable, so they could not do anything to me but I was able to get at them through my art, my writing and simply by being seen as a basically good person by the public. There were some good officers though, particularly Ron the Red, who helped me to embark on writing this book. My sculpting abated and I concentrated on my life story and 'A' levels in sociology and psychology.

Success was intoxicating and, with a parole hearing approaching, I thought I stood a good chance of being released against the judge's recommendation. Even some of the screws told me they thought I would get parole. I waited and waited until, finally, a reply arrived on Christmas Day. The envelope was pushed under my door and I ripped it open eagerly – 'Your parole application has been rejected'. What a Christmas present!

I later found out that the governor, Jock Daley, had received the reply in October but had sadistically decided to withhold it until Christmas Day, to dampen my enthusiasm. I sat with the letter in my hands and felt totally deflated and physically sick. It was painfully obvious what a powerful machine I was fighting against and I was ready to jack it all in. Then, my cell door was opened and in walked the Bishop of Hull, in full clerical regalia. This was so freaky that I actually thought I had been spiked with acid.

I was so shocked that it took me a few minutes to compose myself, after which I confided in the Bishop that I'd just been refused parole. He encouraged me by saying that many people were depending on me and that I should have faith. With that, he departed, leaving me bewildered.

Apparently, he had seen so much about me on television and in the papers that he wanted to meet me in the flesh. When I heard this, I felt proud and, even though I am not a religious man, his words gave me hope, at a time of despair. I just wish I had been better prepared for his visit, so that I could have capitalised on it more effectively.

The staff soon realised that I was far less of a threat when I was sculpting,than when I was writing and a huge lump of beechwood was brought in for me. It is a very tough wood and, as my only tools were a blunt chisel and a slate hammer, it was going to take a long time to carve anything. I thought they must be drunk, if they calculated they could deter me that easily. I attacked the wood like a lunatic, working so frenetically that I cut and bruised myself frequently. I worked like a maniac, often forgetting to eat for days. There was only one thing on my mind and that was completing this sculpture, in as little time possible.

The image I created was of a muscle-bound man supporting a heavily pregnant woman. I wanted to convey the simple message that men are not aware of the complexities of pregnancy and felt that the piece did this quite effectively. I decided that the perfect place to display the piece would be Heddon Road Maternity Hospital, which was just down the road from the prison. I managed to convince the hospital management to take the figure, which I had titled 'Supportive not Oppressive'. My only proviso was that the media would be there, to witness the arrival and unveiling of the work. The huge lump of wood, that was supposed to slow me down, had actually brought me even more exposure so, naturally, I was delighted.

Back on the unit, relations between staff and inmates were deteriorating and I was in the middle of it all. I was constantly being asked to sort out little squabbles, retrieve knives from inmates and generally calm the place down. One time, I had to convince Jacko to release his hostage and, another time, I was called upon to stop Kevo putting chemicals, which he believed were deadly poisons, into the other inmates' tea.

Basically, they were reverting back to their old behaviour but I do not think that this makes the Special Unit a failure. These were the most dangerous and damaged prisoners in the country, some of whom had been in jail for most of their lives. Some had just gone too far to be helped but, even so, I think they benefited from the liberal regime of the unit.

For a start, at least we could have a proper conversation with some of the screws, which had never happened in other prisons. We all learned new skills in the unit and mine helped me change my life but even for someone like Kevo, who will never get out of prison, discovering the ability to paint, was of massive benefit to him personally.

To be treated like a human being and not an animal, may seem like a fundamental right but a hell of a lot of people dismiss dangerous prisoners as worthless. The Special Unit proves that even the most 'evil' men in society do have some good in them, which should be brought out. Rehabilitation in prisons is often criticised for not being sufficiently punitive but to lose your liberty, to have someone else in charge of your life, is one of the worst punishments which can be inflicted on anyone. To deny someone his liberty is often necessary but to deny someone's humanity can never be justified.

In the Special Unit, peer pressure was used to exert discipline, rather than resorting to more punitive methods. This was called positive reinforcement and, basically, involved a lot of discussion between staff and inmates, to work out how the unit should be run. There were no formal rules, only those that we all agreed on and even these were flexible. The better you behaved, the better your treatment and the more privileges you were allowed.

This system promotes sociable behaviour, whereas other prisons use a regime that operates through conflict. As a product of the negative prison system, initially, I could not cope with the lack of confrontation. Just as in Grendon, I tried to create trouble but it is very hard, when the staff are treating you humanely. Eventually, you realise that some of the staff are actually decent blokes. In the past, I had only seen the uniform but I slowly learned to see the man behind it. I also think it was a learning process for many of them, as well. Certainly, in my case, some of the officers began to see beyond the labels which had defined me in the past and began to view me as a person.

Unfortunately, not all the staff were either willing or able to play by the new rules and one particular incident demonstrates how such individuals can destroy so much of the good done by their colleagues. Dave Jackson, one of the probation officers on the unit, was known by everyone as 'Dodgy Dave'. Everything he did had an ulterior motive, usually selfish. We felt he was only interested in his career and that he was only in the unit as it was considered tough work and he had calculated on it getting him a promotion.

The trouble started when I had just returned from Hull Royal Infirmary, after undergoing an appendectomy. I wasn't physically ready to return but I was finding the caring environment in hospital too much of a contrast with prison life, so I discharged myself early. When I got back, I found out that Dodgy Dave had gone beyond his brief and taken some video tapes from my cell, without my permission. Apparently, Fat Fred Low had wanted them, to tape 'Little House on the Prairie'. I was annoyed but had to laugh at the thought of Fat Freddie, the vicious murderer, crying over a shitty, sentimental, television programme.

Accompanied by Ron the Red and Senior Officer Delby, I went and confronted Dodgy Dave. An argument followed during which, I made sure I kept my cool. Suddenly, Dodgy leapt up and started screaming like a woman:

"You have nothing.....you think you're big. You're just shit, you are, just shit and I'm gonna fix you." I remained calm and just told him we should sit down and talk things through.

"After all, I'm supposed to be the psychopath and you're the professional. It isn't good for your image."

Dodgy had flipped and he started squealing. Then off he minced, gibbering nonsense at the staff as he went. Tony Clark, my personal officer, came over to join us.

"What was all that about?" he asked.

"He's gone off his head," we replied, in harmony.

"Fuck him," said Tony, "I couldn't abide the cunt anyway."

Nothing more was said about the matter. The staff had witnessed what had happened and had heard the bollocks Dodgy Dave came out with, so I simply returned to my cell to get on with some work. A short time later, six officers arrived at my cell, all looking downcast. Dodgy had convinced the governor that I had assaulted him and they were under orders to take me to see him. They knew what had really happened and they hated Dodgy as much as me and I could see that they felt uncomfortable, carrying out their orders.

The governor had swallowed Dodgy's bullshit, without hesitation, and already had the paperwork prepared to legitimise a month's solitary in the dreaded Durham Jail. I tried to argue my case, assisted by Ron and Selby. The governor listened and then altered the paperwork to say that, "it could have been perceived by an onlooker that I was thinking of assaulting Probation Officer Jackson".

The dirty bastards were going to put me in solitary for a month because someone 'could have thought' that I was going to attack Dodgy Dave Jackson. Utter bullshit. I spat on the governor and called him the fucker that he was. I was chained up and thrown into a secure van with six staff and then whisked off to Geordie Land.

The injustice of it all was tearing me apart. My precious sculptures and my writing were at Hull. Had all my attempts to mend my ways been pointless? At that moment, everything seemed wasted. It was a huge, retrograde step and, even though the staff at Hull had told me to keep my gob shut, I was going to kick off.

Once the chains were off, I kicked off good-style, throwing plates and furniture around.

"Fucking Geordie maggots. Come and have a bit of me, you fucking cunts," I screamed futilely at them. After a big shake-up, they cuffed me, cut all my clothes off and threw me in the strong box, to cool off for a day.

When it was time to be let out, I got the usual beating and then they took me down to the segregation unit, where I was put in solitary confinement. The Geordie screw who locked me up, told me sneeringly,

"If you're a subversive, then my prick's a sausage...I could fucking eat you for breakfast." With that, he slammed the cell door shut and left me to rot. I felt I was doomed.

After two weeks, my appendectomy began to play up, because of my injuries from the scuffle. They had taken away my medicine and, as no one who cared knew where I was and I wasn't allowed any mail or visits, I was pretty fucked. In the past, I would have wallowed in self-pity but I had progressed and, instead of becoming despondent, my thoughts turned to positive action. I needed writing materials and, after grovelling like a dog for days, I was eventually provided with them.

My first task was to write a letter to Jimmy Boyle, previously dubbed

'Scotland's most dangerous man' but now reformed, after his spell in the Special Unit at Barlinnie in Glasgow. He, too, had discovered art and had made a name for himself with his famous autobiography, 'A Sense of Freedom'. I asked him if his experiences had any parallels with mine and also, if he had any advice for me. Jimmy wasted no time in replying and his letter was really encouraging. I was buzzing. If he could succeed, then so could I.

In his letter, he pledged that, on my return, he would visit the Special Unit with a media entourage. He was going to publicise the unit and make sure my efforts were not wasted. This was amazing. Even though I was locked in solitary confinement, I was still able to carry on my campaign, to bring the truth about Britain's prisons to light.

The Durham screws told me that it was chaos back at the Special Unit in Hull. Out of sympathy for my case, the lads had taken to smashing anything they could lay their hands on, phoning the local media, hunger-striking and throwing shit up the walls. Jacko had even had the initiative to write to the Home Secretary, Kenneth Baker to complain about how unfairly I had been treated. They refused to stop the mayhem until Dodgy Dave Jackson was removed from the unit.

Partly because of what he had done and partly because his life was in danger, it was decided that I should be taken back to the unit and that Dave Jackson should be removed. Apparently, the staff had voted him out, which confirmed his unpopularity.

By this time, I had become very unwell. I had lost a stone in weight and my operation scar was infected. I was relieved to be going back but the illness made it hard to be cheerful. On the journey back, the staff were talkative but some were obviously unhappy with my return, as they felt the system had backed down and compromised their power. They knew I was becoming bigger and bigger but they would soon learn that the best was yet to come.

The lads in the unit gave me a great welcome back. They cleaned the shit off the walls and tidied the place up, while I recuperated. When they had finished, it was time to celebrate and the alcoholic hooch was brought out of its hiding- places. We got drunk and started singing and dancing the can-can around the landings. Staff morale was at an all time low but we didn't care. I was filled of with elation, as I now knew that it was possible to fight the system and win. Violence was not the answer, that was negative and counter-productive. I was going to use positivity and a lot of hard work.

Jimmy Boyle visited a week later and there was massive media coverage, just as he had promised. The Special Unit was revealed to the public and my unjust treatment was brought to light. As a result of all this attention, I was invited to speak at the 'Power Sharing Conference' at Grendon Underwood, on behalf of the convict population. Jimmy Boyle was there, as was Kenneth Baker and many other important people from the world of prisons and prison reform. I spoke with pride and conviction, always keeping in mind that I was an advocate for all the prisoners in the country and I was rewarded with a standing ovation.

On my return from the conference, I discovered that Dodgy Dave Jackson had got his just deserts. The probation service had dispatched him to a rough housing estate in Hull, a definite step down the career ladder. What made it even more ironic was that Dodgy had always gone on about the 'toe rags' on the estates, where he claimed the women were all bleached blonde, foul-mouthed, scrubbers and now he was going to be dealing with them every single day. I can't say I felt sorry for him.

Another piece of encouragement was the result of a recent psychological assessment which stated that I was definitely not mad, just bad but that I was progressing in leaps and bounds and carving out a promising future for myself. The psychologist, Dr David Bolingen, advised that I needed to examine my criminal behaviour and I agreed. The report was concrete recognition by the authorities that I was trying to change.

He apologised for not attending the visit by Jimmy Boyle but told me he hated the man for what he had done to his colleagues years ago and couldn't forgive him. This was coming from a man who was always telling me forget the past and not to bear grudges. He was literally seething with hatred but his mood quickly changed when he started telling me about a new arrival at the Special Unit, called Bruce Childs.

Bruce Childs, or 'Brucey Bab,' as we called him, was one of two men accused of some particularly horrible contract killings. He wore spectacles, had long, grey hair which he always covered with a bandana and used to walk around barefoot. He was reputedly a very talented carpenter and had used the tools of his trade to cut up his victims, before burning them on an open fire, piece by piece. He revelled in showing us newspaper cuttings about his trial and boasted about the huge amounts of money he spent on tools, when he was outside.

Me and Brucey got on quite well and we often had long conversations. He liked to tell me that, when he was burning the bodies, the victims' faces would come at him, out of the fire and he would try and kill them again. He was alright but I always made a mental note never to invite him into my cell.

The next few weeks were uneventful. Life on the unit cracked on as normal and I kept myself busy and got on with my bird, until one morning I heard of a suicide in Hull prison. It suddenly struck me what a common occurrence this was and I immediately set about researching suicide in British jails. I was shocked by the frequency of suicide and felt a strong conviction that my now considerable media influence should be used to highlight this terrible problem.

The young man who had killed himself was called Timothy Garrod. He was a patient in a local mental hospital and he had assaulted a member of staff. It is ridiculous that he was charged with a criminal offence, when he was obviously mentally unstable and he should never have been put into a mainstream prison. Despite a history of suicide attempts, he wasn't put onto fifteen minute watch. The whole case reeked of negligence and the more research I did into the subject, the more similar cases I found.

I decided to organise a seminar and invited members of HALOW,

NACRO, MIND, the Samaritans, the Howard League, New Bridge and the Prison Reform Trust. We compiled our findings and sent them to Judge Stephen Tumim of the prison inspectorate and Lord Justice Woolf. In addition, I wrote a short book, 'Save a Life – Stop a Suicide,' for which there was nationwide demand. The proceeds, plus the money from a video I had made about crime prevention, were donated to the system for educating inmates.

All this work did not go unrecognised and I received letters from various police chiefs around the country, expressing their support for my initiatives. Who would have believed that I would ever be praised by the police? The only other letters I had ever received from them, had been warrants for my arrest!

As I became involved in more and more areas, my workrate increased. There were so many wrongs to be righted and I didn't want to stop until I had at least brought them out into the open. I was working sixteen hours a day and my prominence and influence were growing accordingly.

Another field I became involved in and, still engage in today, is lecturing. I gave my first lecture to sixty law students, in the chapel, at Hull prison. The national press was in attendance, as were the usual Home Office spies. The lecture was a resounding success and it was interesting to give the lawyers of tomorrow an alternative view of prison and the legal system.

Even the other lads on the unit were getting involved in some positive activities in their free time, such as making stuffed toys for the children of single mothers. I was really happy for the first time in ages, especially as I had just passed both my 'A' levels. I was doing fine and the staff were still just as supportive. Ron the Red was as fantastic as ever, as was Steve Dove and all the education staff at Hull. I got in touch with my media contacts and told them about some of the things that were happening in the unit. I felt that it was important that the public understood that not all news from prison is bad news.

Unfortunately, as I was in a Special Unit, there were always going to be 'incidents', simply because of the type of prisoner it housed. Although there were times when everyone got along, there was always the feeling that it was only a matter of time before someone exploded. On this occasion, it was the turn of Brucey Bab, who had had enough of prison life and wanted to take the 'cash option'. This means that you get yourself certified, so you can go to a secure hospital, rather than a jail. Brucey had no chance of getting out of jail alive, so he saw it as a better place to spend his time. He was pushing for a move to Broadmoor, or the 'Laughing Academy' as we knew it.

I was in the art room, working on a sculpture and chatting to Steve Dove, when Brucey appeared at the doorway and beckoned me over. I wandered outside, to find him in a excited mood. He whispered to me that he was going to waste Dovey, to strengthen his case for a transfer. I was no angel but wasting Dovey, simply to appear mad, was a bit lively. I just nodded in agreement and walked back to chat to the unsuspecting Dovey.

This was one bad situation. On the one hand, I couldn't grass on Brucey –

that's the way it is in prison – but, on the other hand, I couldn't let it happen, no matter how dangerous and determined he was. Steve Dove had helped me change my life and I wasn't going to stand by while some fucking psychopath wasted him, so he could go to a cushy prison.

I plugged in the electric drill which was noisy and would cause confusion and left Dovey to drill my sculpture. Minutes later, Fat Freddie Low wandered in and warned me to get out of the room, or I would get it too. That was the final straw. Childs couldn't just go around doing as he liked and he certainly couldn't threaten me. I wasn't one of his ghosts, leaping out of the fire, I was the real thing and if he wanted a bit of me, I would drive the drill right through his demented skull. I might have been starting to reform but this is what life in a high security prison is like and sometimes you have to be the biggest animal to survive.

Brucey charged into the room, picked up a chisel and started to circle the room like a wild cat, stalking its prey.

"Who bought these tools?" he asked.

"I did," replied Dovey, absorbed in his work and completely unaware of the danger he was in.

"That's silly, Dovey, buying your own murder weapon." Dovey looked up and began to laugh nervously. Childs raised the chisel, ready to bring it crashing into my teacher's skull. I grabbed the electric drill and pointed it at Childs like a gun.

"Back, you bastard," I screamed.

Childs was literally shaking with insane, murderous, rage. His eyes were almost bursting from their sockets and his skin was taut and chalk white.

"You cunt... you cunt," he seethed.

With that I lunged towards him, intending to stick the drill right through him but, as I leapt forward, I pulled the plug out of the socket. I knocked the devil to the floor and Childs scrambled hastily out of the room.

"Get out of the class," I yelled at him and he scuttled out, shouting that I was a grass. He slammed the door and I immediately turned to face Steve Dove, who stood stone-still, pallid and trembling, unable to look at me, or to believe the scene that had just been played out before his eyes.

I wanted to say something to him but nothing came out. The old pain and anguish had returned more strongly than ever. The pressure was unbearable and I wanted to stab myself, to let it all out. My head was fucking bursting and I barely noticed the screws who were running round the art room, firing questions at me from all directions and my mind totally blanked out. Silently, I wandered back to my cell and locked myself in for the rest of the day. I didn't go for meals. From time to time, the other inmates brought me cups of tea but no words were exchanged.

Night fell and the moon shone cold and blue through the steel bars of my cell window. I broke down. I was filled with emptiness and frustration at having to stay in this world of shit. I cried and cried but when I woke up in the morning, I knew I had work to do. I was not going to let what had happened the day before stop my progress. I was on a mission and I wasn't going to let a loser like Brucey Bab get in my way.

Later that morning, he was body-belted up and hauled off down to solitary. Dovey, God bless him, had taken a few days off and he left the unit a short time later. This effectively put an end to my art work, so I turned my attention to writing my book and manipulating the media. I was involved in a project with Ian Hunter of Radio Humberside, to raise money for street children in South America. These poor kids are homeless orphans who live underground in the sewers. Governments pretend they don't exist and police death squads are employed to kill them, like the vermin who share their sewers. The tape was used by Radio Cracker, a Christian station, to raise people's awareness of the children's plight.

Tony Clark, my personal officer and the head of the Special Unit, had retired because of his nerves. I think I had certainly contributed to his situation; I am a very demanding person and, although it is unintentional, I am now only too aware of the effect I have on people. The new head of the unit was Ron Oatesfield, an old warhorse but, nevertheless, a man of honesty and integrity. He took over from Tony as my personal officer. His first words to me were short and to the point:

"Alright, Frank, lad, I'm your new personal officer. I can talk and I can fight and you can have a bit of me, any way you like."

I took an instant liking to Ron. He was a Doncaster lad, just like me and, even though we had blazing nose to nose rows if I didn't get my own way, we never held it against each other. In fact, he was actually a great help to me and it was Ron who convinced Cleland House, the Prison Service headquarters that, not only was I safe to be readmitted to mainstream prison, but that I should be rewarded with a low security jail.

Ron suggested that I be moved into the type of low security jail where the inmates are housed in dormitory-style, communal billets. His one concern was that, because I wanked a lot, I might disturb the other inmates. I was still full of fuck: as the prison quack had told me, my testosterone levels were exceptionally high.

"How will you cope, if you need to wank, Frankie lad?" Ron asked me, "You can't just pull it off, in a room full of cons."

"I'd just fuck off to the khazi gov, I'm a robber, not a fucking weirdo," I reassured him.

"You're not a robber, you're a reformed crook, who's now a sculptor and a writer," Ron corrected me.

"Yeah, I guess I am," I smiled.

The Home Office was considering Ron's recommendation that I be moved to a low security jail but I knew that it could be months before anything happened. I kept myself busy with project after project and addressing academics, the media and people from the art world, became an everyday occurrence. I was taking on more than I could handle and, in the end, I became stressed out, refusing to eat and suffering from panic attacks. But when you know you're on to something good, it is hard to stop and I have never been one to do things by half.

As my profile rose, I came into contact with many celebrities and influential people who were interested in my work. Ron the Red's old socialist university pals introduced me to the pop group, The Beautiful South, who were known as the House Martins at that time. They were really interested in the social aspects of my work and we sat around, drinking tea and exchanging experiences. They were smashing people and really down to earth.

Members of Hull's football team paid me a visit and even the famous boxer, 'Prince' Naseem Hamed, popped down to help with some fundraising. He was a really nice lad and, contrary to his public image, he was very humble and unpretentious. I was impressed with how well he looked after his family and his community involvement and it was a pleasure to meet him.

All this exposure was fantastic, as the public were finally waking up to some of the realities of prison life but it was starting to give the Home Office the heebie-jeebies. They realised the pull I had over other convicts and the press and it scared them. There was a general election on the way and prison issues were politically-sensitive at the time. They didn't want me stirring up trouble by revealing the truth about what goes on in Britain's prisons and who could blame them? If people fully appreciated the whole story, they would be shocked and disgusted.

I received a letter from Queen Anne's Gate, asking me to refrain from discussing sensitive subjects with the media. What a cheek! To be honest, I was quite flattered that they felt so threatened by me but there was no way I was going to take any notice of the skinny-arsed bastards. Their concern simply confirmed that I was making an impact and it encouraged me to redouble my efforts. Bruce Childs had been moved out of the unit and a new lad, Paul 'The Snake' Ross, had replaced him. Paul was a skinny, pasty lad from London, doing eighteen years for shooting two innocent people. He got his nickname because he was so small, no bigger than a racing snake. He was openly gay and had been Jacko's lover in another jail, so Jacko was happy as he had a new toy to play with.

Paul, too, hated the system and was very good with the pen. He had come into conflict with the prison authorities many times so, when it came to litigation, he was the business. Paul was a good, front-line man to have in disputes over prisoner's rights and it was useful to have someone with his kind of experience working alongside me.

Not long after Paul arrived on the unit, I was informed that I was being transferred to Ranby Prison, a low security jail in Yorkshire. Perhaps the authorities thought that if they moved me away from the high-profile Special Unit, I would have less of a voice. Not a chance! I was determined to exploit the relatively relaxed environment to the full.

Ron Oatesfield came over to say farewell.

"If you fuck up this time, Frankie, it's no return. They'll pack you off to Parkhurst or Broadmoor and you'll never see the light of day again. But I believe in you, you can do well, kid, so give it your best shot."

"Yeah, I will," I replied, feeling a little sad and a little frightened. The Special Unit was the best time I had done and the progress I had made there amazed everyone, including myself. Even the screws had got to like me but, beyond the unit, there was widespread hatred for me amongst screws. My reputation would go before me and I fully anticipated a hard time but bollocks to them. I had purpose in my life and a few, poxy, vindictive bastards were not going to stop me.

When the media found out about the transfer, a press conference was called and the general consensus was that Ranby was too good for me. 'Soft Option for Hard Man', ran one headline. They felt I should have been sent to neighbouring Rampton Prison, a higher security jail. But the inmates and staff on the unit were pleased and their opinion was all that mattered to me. My departure was quite emotional, both for me and the lads, but I had to go. The move was another step away from my past and, therefore, a step in the right direction.

Category 'C' Convict

On arrival at Ranby, I went through the usual reception process. Two lifers, completing the last stint of their sentences, came into the reception area, to see what was going on. Once I was checked in, the reception screw helped me load my paperwork onto a barrow. He handled it like it was dog shit, probably because he knew that a lot of the documents contained criticisms of prisons and prison staff.

Begrudgingly, he helped me but it was obvious that it was almost killing him. Eventually, he couldn't contain himself any longer and he blurted out,

"I can cope with robbers, rapists and murderers but one thing that gets right up my nose, is an intelligent con!" I didn't respond to this unprovoked outburst, just gave him a pitying and understanding look. I genuinely felt sorry for this smallminded, blinkered little man. He was so uneasy around me and only too eager to despatch me to my billet.

"Right kid, you're in Billet B9, up there, around the corner, turn left, then right..."

The place made me feel confused and disorientated. I had been confined in a tiny, concrete submarine for the last three years and the amount of open space in this place was intimidating. It looked exactly like a prisoner of war camp, with wooden billets everywhere and a large security fence, to keep us all in. I set off to find my billet but my body wouldn't budge. A screw looked at me, a little puzzled,

"You're the kid from the Special Unit, aren't you?" he asked, not unkindly.

"Yeah," I replied, feeling embarrassed.

"I understand," he said "you get on and I'll follow you."

The presence of a screw restored a feeling of normality. On the unit, there were at least two screws in attendance everywhere you went and I didn't feel complete without one on my shoulder. As we walked through the prison grounds, I was amazed at the low level of security. I almost laughed at how easy it would be to scale the fence and I couldn't believe that there weren't the usual screws being dragged round by fucking great Alsatian dogs. Although to most people this might appear to be a normal prison, to me it seemed like a holiday camp.

The billet was basically a portacabin, with rows and rows of beds in it. There was very little privacy and it was clear that tension could easily arise in such a setting. I sat on my bed and waited for the lads I would be living with to return from labour. It was a little intimidating when a sea of convicts swept past me, each one taking a good look at me. Some were speaking in Cant, the gypsy language that I could remember from my childhood. The lad who occupied the next bed was actually a gypsy called Kennel. This wasn't his real name but gypsy slang for a house and he was notorious for robbing houses.

Kennel was from a gypsy camp, not far from the jail and, when we talked, it was always in Cant. Despite some feelings of ambiguity about my background, I have always had a certain amount of pride in my gypsy roots, so it was nice to speak in the gypsy tongue but it was also useful, as the other inmates could not understand what we were saying. He called me 'Mushy', another gypsy name. I hadn't mixed in gypsy circles since I was a young boy but it is something that sets you apart from other people and certainly pushed me and Kennel together.

When night came, we all had to be counted and so we stood to attention at the end of our beds while a screw went round checking if everyone was there. Unfortunately, the screw was a stupid cunt who couldn't count properly. The piss pot parade seemed to go on for a lifetime. When it was over, most of the lads just chilled out. Most took drugs, some read, wrote letters and one group bullied people and fought amongst themselves. Everyone was listening to personal stereos. It was really weird. I had been in prisons for twenty-four years of my life but I had never come across anything like this.

After a while, most people started showering off and going to bed. That first night seemed endles. I was restless and couldn't sleep due to the noise and various activities going on in the dormitory. Radios were left on and several of the lads cried because they knew someone's tattie was up their girlfriend. Some tried to masturbate discreetly, others didn't give a fuck who saw them. A kangaroo court was going on at the bottom of the billet, with cons playing judge, jury and executioner to some little scrap who hadn't paid for the heroin he'd used. It was horrendous and, as the rain rattled on the fibreglass roof, I drifted into an uneasy slumber.

When I awoke the next morning, the sun was shining and I felt far more positive.

"I will get through," I repeated to myself, over and over again. Most of the lads were still snoring and waking them up would have caused a confrontation. They were pussycats compared to the types I was used to being banged up with but I didn't want to get mobile here, especially as it was only my second day. I was desperately trying to leave all that behind me.

The dining-room was miles away and, as the food was of the normal pig shit standard, it hardly seemed worth the effort. Kennel seemed to love his food and he couldn't wait to get down there.

"Roll on, Mushy, if you want your scran," he said, encouraging me to walk faster.

However, his initial friendliness changed over night. In fact, every inmate in the prison refused to speak to me. This was quite eerie and it took me a while to figure out what the problem was.

It transpired that, as I had anticipated, many of the staff were not happy to have me in their jail. They decided to tell the inmates that I had just arrived from a hospital for the criminally insane, that I was a dangerous psychopath and warned them all to be on their guard. I was confused; the prison service had tried to help me to reform and, when I showed signs of doing that, they tried to undermine me. It was also a very ill-advised game to play, as it frightened the convicts and, when convicts get frightened, they get violent. Then, if they can't deal with it alone, they deal with it together. Maybe they wanted me to get done in but there was no way I was going to let that happen, especially by the two-bit criminals in Ranby.

I'd spent most of my time in prison with the worst villains imaginable and now, here I was, being sent to Coventry by a bunch of pathetic sods who listened to the bollocks fed to them by the screws. I didn't expect them to respect me or anything, it just seemed odd that these men were prepared to turn against me so readily, just because the men who locked them up had told them to. I was fighting their corner for fuck's sake and all they could do was act like sheep and do exactly what the system wanted. It made me despair of them but the screws really must have misjudged me, or have been thicker than they looked, if they thought they could break me that easily.

In my head, I reversed the situation. I told myself that instead of them blanking me, I was blanking them. I was worried that I was going to get attacked and, even though I had vowed never to be violent again, it was a question of me or them. I sawed off a metal bed leg and carried it with me at all times. I looked unflinchingly into the eyes of anyone who attempted to stare me out. This shower of shit would soon realise that I wouldn't be intimidated by their feeble efforts.

I was ready to kick the shit out of anyone who fronted me, although Ron Oatesfield's last words to me in the Special Unit were still fresh in my head and I desperately didn't want to fuck up. I decided to use my brains a bit more and employ some slightly more subtle methods. I deliberately left photocopies of my media coverage lying around, knowing that the nosey bastards on the billet wouldn't be able to resist looking at them. This would make them realise that I wasn't a headcase and that I was actually fighting for the rights of prisoners. Also, the fact that I was once described as South

Yorkshire's most dangerous gunman would also make them think twice about trying to waste me.

As planned, the inmates were fascinated. Many of them came over to apologise for the way they had treated me and most were interested in my past and my projects in the Special Unit. Their disrespect turned to admiration and it was apparent that, even if I had been at the prison for three years, I couldn't have made so many friends. It was all down to the good work I had accomplished, which again reinforced my belief in myself.

I landed the job of billet cleaner, one of the best you can get in prison. I would rush up and down the billet every morning, mopping and sweeping in double quick time, so that I would have the rest of the day free to work on my writing. The educational support I required was not forthcoming and I wasn't allowed to further my education in any way. The Special Unit had relied on positive reinforcement but here the regime was strictly negative.

However, the atmosphere was much more relaxed than that of other prisons I had experienced, so I was able to develop a relationship with someone in the education department. She was literally the sexiest woman I had ever met and I thought about her all the time. I ached when I couldn't see her but it was better than having to wank all the time, which was what good old Ron was so worried about. I wonder if he would have approved of the way I got round that little problem! This lady also made sure I had all the pens and paper I needed to carry on with my work.

While in Ranby, I was contacted by a man called Eric McGraw, head of the long-established charity for prisoners, New Bridge. He wanted me to speak at their annual youth conference, on the subject of crime and punishment. Eric had taken the initiative to clear it with the Home Office and also Bill Abbot, the governor of Ranby. Naturally, I accepted his offer without hesitation.

The conference was in Manchester and I was allowed to travel down the night before. I stayed in a posh hotel in the city centre, where I met many of famous and interesting people who were speaking at the conference. One of these was Sir Charles Erving, who used to be an MP in Gloucestershire. He was heavily involved with New Bridge and he was a very caring, sensitive man. We corresponded regularly for some time but, sadly, he recently passed away. I also made many other friends in New Bridge, who have continued to help and support me.

The conference went really well. I was speaking after Dr Susan Edwards of the Metropolitan Police and David Jessel, who presents programmes about miscarriages of justice. They were both shared a strong desire to raise social awareness. My speech was well appreciated and, again, it was satisfying to be in a position to give prisoners a voice.

After the conference, I was inundated with requests to speak in prisons, schools, colleges and universities about various issues related to crime and imprisonment and my personal experiences of them. I was more than willing to attend them all. I enjoyed giving the talks and they always seemed to be appreciated, which indicated that my message was getting through. In addition, they gave me a chance to get away from Ranby, which was a blessing indeed.

The best of these conferences was organised by Sir Richard Storey, the High Sheriff of North Yorkshire, who invited me to speak at Sterling House in Malton. The audience was made up of important figures from the world of the police and prisons, so it was an ideal opportunity to directly target the people who mattered. Speaking alongside me was Gilbert Grey QC, Lord Wetherhill and Roy King, a lecturer at York University.

I was only scheduled to speak for thirty-five minutes but my comments were so well-received that I talked for an hour and a half. At the end, I was given a standing ovation, which made me feel very proud. Lord Wetherhill sent me a letter, thanking me for speaking, which read as follows:

"I do not think I need to tell you how well your comments were received. There is no doubt that you outshone the rest of us in your ability to speak from practical experience and from the heart..."

That a member of the House of Lords could be so impressed with my speaking was a huge boost. It also meant that an important politician actually believed in what I said, which was more pleasing to me than anything else.

Sir Richard Storey also wrote a similar letter, as did some of the judges, lords, MPs, lawyers, police chiefs, governors, probation officers and clergymen who also attended the conference. It was a milestone in my campaign but, at the same time, it left me feeling rather strange. Here I was, hobnobbing with members of the establishment one minute and the next, I was back in jail, locked up with a load of crooks. It was very bewildering but exciting at the same time.

The number of functions I was attending was astonishing and I was out of prison, as much as I was in it. This served to fuel the staff's hatred of me even further, especially as the inmates had put me up as their leader. They started tampering with my mail and some of the lads informed me that the screws had offered them bribes to beat me up and plant drugs in my belongings, so I could be fitted up. So this was the constant dilemma I was facing. While I was in prison, I was convict Cook, the gunman and armed robber, who was serving out the remainder of his sentence but, when I was lecturing, I was Mr Cook, authority on crime, punishment and prison reform. As a convict, I was subjected to all the sly digs from the screws, together with all the general stress of living, cheek by jowl, in a billet full of criminals. The reality of my situation was in direct conflict with the person who I aspired to be and, on the outside, was actually becoming. I frequently worried that I was losing my identity and I was constantly stressed out.

I wrote to some of the influential people I now knew, telling them that, although Ranby was a low security jail, gratuitous and senseless violence was not stopped and was sometimes even encouraged. The staff were aggressive, there was no sense of direction for inmates and there was a chronic heroin problem. Needless to say, the screws hated me even more after making these revelations but it made me happy. To be hated by them was a fine accolade.

It was now autumn and my birthday had come around. I had totally forgotten, as it was something that I had rarely celebrated. This year was different though: the lads had decided to throw a surprise party for me and had used the bedsheets to make banners saying 'Free Frank Cook' and 'Happy Birthday', as a mark of gratitude, for fighting for their rights. I was overwhelmed but quickly realised the trouble it would cause. They had done it with the best intentions but it was sure to antagonise the staff and certainly make me even less popular with them, if that was possible. Everybody refused labour that day and the booze and drugs were brought out. All the lads were having a great time and Kennel was running about shouting, "Free Frank Cook", and telling me to get some 'peave', the gypsy slang for alcohol, down my throat.

Later on, I was pretty pissed and, after smoking a few spliffs, I was feeling great. Unfortunately, I enjoyed smoking the cannabis so much, that I started having a regular spliff each night, to relieve the stress I was feeling. One spliff soon turned into a few and, before long, I was smoking far too much. The infirmary only offered me paracetamol for the stress, so cannabis became my medication and then, nearly my damnation. My brain started to function more slowly, I couldn't concentrate and inevitably my work suffered.

Although I was very popular amongst the lads at Ranby, none of them understood me properly and I felt mentally and emotionally isolated. Of course, I was pleased with my success but it had turned me into something of a media commodity. Everyone knew a different Frank Cook but I was just a con, feeling lonely and I really didn't think I deserved to be in prison anymore. Most people would have had parole by now for good behaviour but I had not just been good, I was a shining example of how the prison service can actually help a criminal to reform and better himself. However, I consoled myself, I had another parole application coming up shortly and most people were sure I would be released soon.

The reply to my parole application came back and it was yet another knock-back. It stipulated that I was to serve the full term of my sentence, another three years, in Rudgate Open Prison. Basically, they had given me a move to a better prison but kicked me in the bollocks at the same time. The mind games were continuing. They knew I was a threat to them, so they couldn't treat me too badly but wanted to disrupt my progress as much as possible.

The atmosphere at Ranby turned hostile. People were saying that if a model prisoner like me couldn't get parole, what chance did they have? To relieve the tension, I was quickly whisked away to Rudgate Prison in West Yorkshire. It was the worst move of my prison life, as I knew that the establishment was firmly against me and I had virtually no hope of an early release.

I was confronted at the gates of Rudgate by the governor, whose name I didn't even care to find out. He made it very clear to me that I was unwelcome in his jail, which came as no surprise. He spitefully informed me that the only reason he was accepting me was that his orders came from people in high places and he then proceeded to dish out the usual macho bullshit about how I would "...most certainly have a bit of him," but I just switched off; I'd heard it all before, so many times. Right now, I was stressed out and dying for a spliff.

I was back on home turf now and, consequently, was known by a lot of the lads in the jail. I was a big man in there and even the cons who didn't know me had heard about my reputation, or had seen me on the box. Booze and drugs were plentiful and, as the papers reported, women were often sneaked into the jail. Despite drinking heavily and taking drugs to relax, I maintained my high workrate, concentrating on various media items and continuing to lecture frequently. Again, I found myself acting like a counsellor for many of the inmates, who would come to me with their little worries. It was a difficult time and my nerves were in tatters. I wasn't eating properly and weight was dropping off me. They had really succeeded in fucking me up with this last move.

My room-mate was Billy 'Liar' Burns, a lifer from Leeds, whom I'd met many times in various top security prisons. He had a problem with telling the truth and nearly everything that came out of his mouth was pure bullshit. He was also well-known as the prison grass and, needless to say, he was not the most popular person with the other inmates. He talked incessantly about trivia and he really did my head in, although, as a long-termer like me, I always held out some sympathy towards him. The other lads advised me to boot him out but I didn't have the heart, even though he was the last person I wanted to share a room with.

Day after day, other long-termers would arrive to finish off their sentences and it was like an old lags reunion. Most of them I had known when they were young and it was depressing to see that now, they were almost all, broken, damaged men. Just as in Ranby, all the cons loved me but the staff despised me and did everything in their power to piss me right off. Whatever I asked for, I was refused. My mail was tampered with and I was frequently woken up in the middle of the night, sometimes by having a bucket of cold water thrown over me. Billy said we should get hooded up and batter the bastards but I knew violence was not the answer. I still held out faint hopes of parole and wouldn't entertain anything that would jeopardise it.

My health had deteriorated even more and was now pretty poor and Billy kept badgering me to go to the doctor's. At first, I pretended I was alright but, when I looked in the mirror, I could see that I looked tired and drawn and that I was losing it. I finally gave in, when I slipped and badly twisted my knee. The doctor was totally unsympathetic and he refused to send me to hospital. He said there was nothing wrong with me and that I didn't need treatment. I was given a pair of crutches and told to get on with it.

In prison, you can't request a second opinion, so my only option was to hobble around the jail as best I could. All was well, until I attempted to collect my meal tray. Obviously, my hands were taken up with the crutches, so I looked helplessly around the dining-room for help. A young Asian lad jumped up eagerly and offered to assist me but, as he went to pick up my tray, a fat screw hollered from the other side of the room:

"Hey! Abdul, leave that tray alone. Don't let me see anyone help that man." He looked at me, unsure what to do.

"Thanks Gralez, just leave it," I said. Gralez was his real name. The screws only called him Abdul because they were a bunch of racist bastards and that was their idea of a joke.

Some of the inmates thought the screw was funny, mostly the white-collar, first-time offender types. They would get eaten alive in two seconds flat in a regular jail and I despised these sycophantic bastards, who licked the screws' arses. I was determined to show them that I was no fool to be laughed at. I let both crutches drop, grabbed the tray and started hopping over to a table but I lost my balance and fell. I lay, spread-eagled on the floor, the spilt food scattered all around me, unable to get up because of my bad knee. Some of the cons were laughing and jeering and I was completely humiliated and embarrassed. Billy ran over to help me, screeching abuse at the inmates who were laughing.

"You fucking short-term, bed and breakfast bastards. You think you're fucking crooks but you'd cry in the jails we've been in, you shower of shit."

Instantly, the room went silent, as the cowardly cunts realised that it would be unwise to find themselves on the wrong side of people like Billy and me. By now, I was feeling quite emotional and, in my head, I knew I was losing it. I was a shadow of the man I'd been a few months ago and the dirty tricks campaign was succeeding in undermining my self-esteem. I wrote to my friend, Sir Charles Erving, to let him know I was struggling. I needed his advice and also wanted him to find out if there was a possibility that I would ever get parole.

He offered me encouragement but his letter also contained some ominous news from the Parole Board. Sir Charles had written to them, enquiring about me and he had enclosed their reply in his letter. It read as follows:

"No matter how well Frank Cook has done, transcending everything that has been required of him, he will still have to serve every day of his sentence. Regarding seeing the Parole Board, I'm afraid Mr Cook is barking up the wrong tree. His papers are not viewed by the Parole Board, as inmate Cook is under ministerial scrutiny and his applications for parole are immediately refused and sent back."

The document was from the Queen Anne's Gate, Home Office Headquarters. My fate was sealed. My next three years were going to be spent in a shitty open prison with my head battered. The prospect of it was nearly enough to flip me out and that night I was unable to sleep. As I lay awake, I thought that if I could just take a break from the madness, I would be able to get my head together.

On the Run

Soon after receiving Sir Charles' letter, I was due to address students at the Lawnswood School in Leeds. When I lectured, I no longer had to travel with a screw, as the prison service deemed that I had too high a profile for me to effect an escape.

The students were very receptive and, in return, I put everything into my talk. These people are the professionals of tomorrow and I took great pride in giving them something of value. The head teacher was especially pleased and I have since lectured at the school again. The lecture over, it was time to get the train back to Rudgate but I wasn't going back. My head would have exploded if I had returned at that point and I needed a holiday to sort myself out.

My brother, Vincent, picked me up and handed me my passport, airline tickets to Spain and a bundle of money. Vinny's flashy Ford Cosworth spirited us down to the East Midlands Airport but, as we got nearer, my apprehension was building. Would I get nicked boarding the plane? Rudgate shouldn't have been missing me yet, so I was probably going to be alright.

Once I was through airport security and ready to board the plane, I used a mobile phone to call the governor of Rudgate. I told him that I was going on holiday and that I'd send him and the Home Secretary a postcard. I told him it wasn't personal and that I'd give myself up, when I had chilled out.

"Cookie, lad, come back and we can talk about this," he pleaded with me.

"Better still, Guv, I can use the mobile phone to talk to you while I'm lying on the beach, getting a sun tan and I'll even reverse the charges...Bye for now."

I boarded the plane, the adrenaline kicking in and with no regrets whatsoever. We touched down in Marbella and, as I stepped off the plane, I could literally feel the stench of prison leaving my nostrils. Over the next few days, all I did was eat, drink and sleep. It was pure relaxation and the only thing I did, was phone up the press every so often, basically taking the piss. Doncaster Police had issued a warning that I should return to jail, or I would be in serious trouble. A lot of people who had wanted to see me fail, were delighted and they came out and slagged me off but I didn't give a toss.

Drinking in a bar one day, I recognised a girl I knew from England. She was called Jackie and was an ex-model from Birmingham. She was no angel and was known as the 'Queen of Brum' by the Birmingham underworld but she was very attractive and, although she had just got over a divorce, we hit it off straight away. It was all so romantic that I was overwhelmed and we decided to get married but I didn't confess to her that I was on the run. We flew back to England together and obtained a special licence for a 'quickie' marriage in the Midlands.

All sorts of villains from all over England turned up to see us get married but I was already starting to have misgivings. The ceremony itself was terrifying, far worse than being in the dock. Before I knew it, I was married.

So it was champagne and cocaine all round and off to the Lake District for the honeymoon.

I had allowed myself to get completely carried away in Spain. The classic, heady combination of sun, sand, sea and sex, had contrasted so starkly with prison life that it had captivated me, as if I was a teenager let loose on holiday for the first time. But now I was back in England, the full reality of my predicament hit me like a sledgehammer and I realised the gravity of my situation. The police were still appealing for me to come back and now I had the additional complication of a wife to deal with. I didn't really want to be married, so I allowed her to find out that I was an escaped convict. She went ballistic and smashed up the hotel room and then started on me. After she had cooled down, she declared her undying love for me and promised she would wait for me to get out of jail.

She didn't understand the full implications of what lay ahead and I knew that she wouldn't be able to wait three years for me to get out. I felt trapped and I hated it. I actually wanted to be back in prison but the thought of that frightened me as well. The prospect of having the shit kicked out of me was very real and I would possibly have to spend the rest of my sentence in isolation. I was worried about what would happen to me when I first gave myself up, so I contacted the media to make sure they were present when it happened.

I enjoyed a last pint, posed for photographs for the Daily Mail and then turned myself in at Bridlington Police Station. My fears turned out to be well-founded. Instead of being sent back to Rudgate, I was shunted from jail to jail, always in isolation. By escaping, I had played into their hands and had given them the perfect excuse to try and break my spirit and, although I couldn't afford to let them see it, they were succeeding. I had no choice but to protest; in Leicester prison, the seventeenth jail in a matter of months, I went on hunger strike.

After a month without food, the governor came to see me and, although he was at pains to hide it in my presence, he was genuinely concerned. He told me that my situation was out of his hands and even admitted that he, personally, didn't think I should still be in prison. He pledged that he would move me at the drop of a hat but his orders came from above and that I must have got up some minister's nose. I told him that all I wanted was a jail I could settle down in and get my head down for the rest of my sentence and that, if he could get me moved, I would terminate my hunger strike.

He agreed that if I terminated my fast, he would try his best to get me moved but there was no guarantee that he would be successful. This guy was alright and I trusted him, so I tried to eat but it had been twenty-nine days since my last meal and I just couldn't physically do it. I had developed a form of anorexia and so they put me on the hospital wing whilst I recuperated. Luckily, I was still in isolation, as 'One Flew Over the Cuckoo's Nest' had nothing on the cases in this hospital.

One bloke thought he was a frog, one thought he was a telephone and another poor soul was convinced he was the Road Runner. In the middle of the night they all kicked off:

"Ribbet, ribbet, drring, drring, meep, meep," all night long.

"I've heard everything now," I thought to myself. All I had to do was dance around my cell doing the Monster Mash and get the governor down to do a ballet dance; then we had an entire fucking roadshow. The tragedy of it all was not lost on me but I couldn't help laughing; something I hadn't done since my return to prison.

Transfer to Stocken

Governor Ross, from Leicester, was as good as his word and he managed to secure me a transfer to Stocken Prison. I arrived early in the morning and was immediately processed and located on A Wing. I wasn't allocated any work and that meant bang up all day, so, when I noticed a poster advertising a course in creative writing, I enrolled straight away.

The class was full of the usual assortment of odds and sods and we all competed for the attention of the very attractive class tutor, Michaela Morgan. She was an excellent teacher and she would do anything she could to help and support her little band of criminals but she would not take any nonsense and we all respected her. The other staff often warned her about being alone in a room full of dangerous villains but she was not worried and we never caused her any problems.

A Liverpool lad, called Robert Smith, was one of the better writers in the group and he had written his autobiography, which was later published. This gave me the inspiration to continue with my book and generally get back to my old, industrious ways. The class was the most important thing to me and, if it was ever cancelled, I would get very depressed. It was my only form of mental stimulation and it stopped me from causing trouble out of sheer boredom.

My hasty, ill-advised marriage to Jackie was doomed from the start. Despite her promises, she only visited me once while I was back inside and, after she told me she was pregnant and that the child was not mine, we decided to put an end to it, as soon as possibe. She filed for divorce, on the grounds that I was a convicted felon who was mentally unstable and that she was carrying another man's child. We also both agreed to her claiming that the marriage had not been consummated, as we felt that this would speed up the legal process. As far as I know, she joined the baby's father, to live happily ever after.

My dreams of going straight were fading fast and it seemed like all my achievements had come to nothing. What was the point in striving and doing well, when it just resulted in the authorities picking on me? I had no motivation to be a villain again but then, somewhere along the way, I had lost my powerful motivation to go straight. Being a villain entailed hassle, worry and always having to look over your shoulder but it also meant cash. I knew it was wrong and I still lectured about the evils of crime nearly every week but the old, fatalistic, negative thoughts began to re-enter my head. This line of thinking was insidiously seductive and I started to feel convinced that there was nothing I could do to escape crime so I might as well give in. The optimism, which had filled the last few years, now seemed based on false hope. Whilst I still believed strongly in everything I had talked or written about, I was no longer convinced that I was the one to get the message across.

I began to tell the inmates and staff that I was as unrepentant as ever and that I had not reformed. Many of the prisoners were pleased, because a crook like me provided a role model for them and the staff were actually jubilant; their scepticism and prejudices had been proved right. My relationship with them was now firmly back on terms which they understood: I gave them shit, they gave me shit back. Cons were all bad in their eyes and, when I had started to do worthwhile things, it had confused the issue and they couldn't deal with me. Now I was a self-confessed crook again, they felt comfortable, as it reaffirmed all their blinkered beliefs. The vicious cycle of bickering and violence erupted again and I quickly slid deeply into the thick of it. It had taken me years of sustained effort to climb out of it but only a matter of days, to be sucked back in.

Consequently, it came as huge shock when I was informed that I was being released nineteen months prior to the end of the full seven years. When I had been behaving impeccably, I was told I had absolutely no chance of parole. Now I had confessed to be unreformed and I was being released. It was wrong and I wanted to speak out about the irony of it all but that would only have embroiled me in more trouble and I was just overjoyed to be finally getting out of prison.

Freedom

Waiting for me outside the jail, in a huge white Mercedes, was my cousin Deano and his mate, Gazza. They got out of the car with big grins plastered on their faces and came over to embrace me. Both of them were drug dealers and the staff watching, knew it as well as I did. Deano cracked open a bottle of bubbly and shoved a fat cigar into my mouth.

"Nice to see you, Franko, I've been hearing good things about you," he winked, ostentatiously pouring me a glass of champagne.

"Cop a look at this, Franko," Deano said, opening the boot of the car. Inside, was a neat pile of designer clothes and, to the left, was a revolver and some ammo.

"That shooter doesn't come with the clobber, does it?" I joked, laughing nervously. I always knew Deano was a cocky bastard and had the reputation for being a bit sloppy but the sight of a gun in the car I was driving away from prison in was a bit rich. This, and the little display they had just put on, confirmed my opinion that today's young villains are just as egocentric and unrealistic as ever. They have no understanding of what carrying a gun entails and are a danger to themselves and the public. It also made me realise that my biggest problem on being released was that everyone I knew was a crook.

The public had begun to see me as Frank Cook, the reformed villain and, in their minds, I was naturally going to come out of prison and walk straight into a respectable job. Unfortunately, it is not like that in the real world. It is virtually impossible for ex-cons to get jobs, especially ones who have been inside as long as me. Who in their right mind would employ someone who has a criminal record, when they could just as easily employ someone who doesn't?

Even though I had recently told people in prison that I was totally unreformed, that was not true. I had undergone an enormous transformation over the last five years and I now felt worlds apart from Deano and Gazza. What I desperately wanted was a normal job, so that I could settle down and live a decent life but, if that didn't happen, then I was not going to be poor. I couldn't exist on the pittance the government hands out to you but, without crime, I would have to. My head was spinning as the old problems, which I thought I had dealt with, came flooding back into my brain.

When I had inspected the clothes, we jumped into the flashy motor and screeched out of the prison car park. The sour-faced screws looked on in disgust and we all laughed derisively as we flew past them. We sped off down the motorway until we reached a Little Chef, where we stopped for a massive breakfast. While Gazza went off to order and pay for the food, Deano slipped me a large brown envelope and whispered in my ear,

"It's good to get you out of that shit heap, Franko. Cop for this." The envelope was stuffed with cash, which, of course, was exactly what I needed but taking charity was not my style.

As we travelled north to Doncaster, the conversation inevitably turned to the usual gangster topics. This was the way I used to talk but, because of my experiences in the Special Unit, it now made me feel strangely uncomfortable. I wanted to distance myself from my old life but it still held a certain allure. Everything that had happened over the last few years had been exciting and refreshing but it was still frighteningly new. As Deano and Gazza chatted away, it all seemed so familiar and that made me feel secure. A conflict was raging within me and I could feel myself being pulled relentlessly back towards the criminal world.

The next two weeks were spent partying, meeting old friends and talking to the media. My head was whirling, just like it always did after release and, to top things off, I was now getting offers of bits of 'work'. Being back in Balby was definitely not doing my prospects of staying straight any good, so it was a relief when I had to go down to Birmingham, to meet my parole officer.

At our first meeting, it was instantly apparent that she couldn't abide me. Her hostility was barely-disguised by her professional politeness and I was very glad that I would only have to meet her once a week. With the interview complete, I was allowed to go to my new residence, the Little Crown Pub, owned by some of Birmingham's top villains and she knew, as well as I did, that this was a ridiculous and cynical place to send me.

At the Little Crown I was greeted by plenty of my old pals and we soon got down to a serious drinking session. The booze flowed freely, as did the cocaine and the weed. These people were rolling in money from the proceeds of crime and they were certainly not tight with it. After days of partying, I began to envy their lifestyle and greed quickly got the better of my good intentions. I, too, wanted a piece of the action, so I telephoned Deano in Nottingham and asked him to come down to Birmingham, to meet me, to sort out some work.

What Deano had lined up for me was a forty-seven thousand pound cannabis deal. He wanted me to arrange the deal with my Brummie mates, who would supply the cannabis, which Deano would then come down and pay for. Setting up the deal was no problem and the drugs were delivered swiftly to Nottingham by one of the Brummie's footsoldiers, on the understanding that he would pay for them within the next four days.

Deano had only given me a measly fifty quid for sorting the deal and, when there was no sign of him after four days, I began to get really pissed off. The Brummies were breathing down my neck, so I set off for Nottingham to sort everything out. I found Deano lounging in his house, with his mum and dad and the whole of his firm. When I told him that the Brummies were getting very annoyed, he just laughed.

"You saw the Daimler outside, didn't you, Frank? That's yours and here's nineteen grand. The Brummies aren't getting paid." For once, I was speechless.

"Don't worry, Franco," Deano reassured me, "this is how it goes in the drug game. You need a rip-off from time to time. You've always been a robber and it's all new to you." He was right. This was a million miles away from the kind of thing I used to get up to. I was out of touch but my pride told me that anything these kids could do, I could do as well.

Taking the new motor, I travelled round the country, visiting various friends and acquaintances. The Brummies held me totally responsible for the loss of the drugs and the word on the street was that they were going to shoot me, if they caught up with me. Cat and mouse games went on for three weeks and, by now, I was armed and totally immersed in criminality once more. The progress I had made in the Special Unit was now a distant memory, which I deliberately suppressed. I pretended to myself that I had tried to go straight but, in the back of my mind, I knew that I hadn't really made any kind of serious attempt. If I am honest with myself, the conflict with the Brummies excited me and made me feel important.

Eventually, the Birmingham mob tired of the whole business and the trouble fizzled out. I spent a couple of weeks relaxing in Doncaster and then travelled down to South London to meet my friend Petra, a member of the New Bridge organisation, who had asked me to accompany her to the Tate Gallery. As I drove down there, I deliberated the contradictions that made up my personality. I was going to London to appreciate fine art whilst, only the day before, I had been driving about with a gun in my boot. There were two distinct sides to me: the old Frank Cook who was a selfish, violent thug and the new Frank Cook who sculpted, wrote and rejected criminal activities. I tried to establish, once and for all, which one was the true me and realised that the only time I had been truly happy was when I had been doing good and helping other people. I liked the money and enjoyed the glamorous lifestyle that went with being a gangster but it didn't satisfy me. My current goals were false ones but it was so hard to throw off my past and I persuaded myself that I had no other choice.

On arrival in London, I phoned the West Midlands Probation Service, to tell them where I was and enquire when they next wanted to see me. To my horror, the woman on the other end of the line, Mrs. Brown, Senior Probation Officer, told me that they didn't want to see me at all; I had been recalled to prison and was now unlawfully at large and should report to the nearest police station. No reason was given and I certainly hadn't been arrested, so I didn't know what the hell was going on. Petra said she would accompany me to Belgravia Police Station and I was glad to have someone who understood the way the police worked, in my corner.

At the station, I strode straight up to the front desk and announced why I was there. They asked me to confirm my identity and then glanced at Petra, who nodded in agreement. As soon as they knew who I was, all hell broke loose. Armed police, in bullet-proof jackets, leapt over the desk and pinned me to the floor. With brutal efficiency, I was handcuffed and whisked off to the cells. As I was dragged off, I looked back to see Petra, leaning casually against the front desk, with a smile on her face. I was puzzled that she should seem so nonchalant about such an alarming situation but I later discovered that she had known what was going on all along and had agreed to help bring me in.

After a few hours in the cells in Belgravia, I was taken to Brixton Prison and placed on the wing for the criminally-insane. There was no reception procedure, which is very unusual and I was thrown straight into a padded cell. Before long, they hauled me out again and I was interviewed for what seemed like hours. The only reason I could find for me being dragged back to jail was a visit I had made to a psychiatrist from Birmingham's Rayside Secure Unit, just after my release, five weeks ago. She had assumed, without foundation, that I was a serial killer or, if not, that I certainly had the potential to be one. She may have been influenced by her experiences of the previous eleven months, which she had spent interviewing Fred West. She had apparently alerted the police to her conviction that I was both insane and very dangerous, so I was recalled. I was interviewed by psychiatrists from Broadmoor, Rampton and Park Lane and each of them agreed that I was very much in sound mind but possibly still dangerous. They were right but this was still not a sufficient reason for bringing me back in, when I hadn't committed another crime, or, at least, not one that the police were aware of. I was then put on normal location, where I continually demanded an official explanation for my continued detainment.

I was made to serve out the nineteen months that had originally been taken from my sentence. Although it was a crushing blow at the time, with hindsight, it was a blessing in disguise. The unfairness of my treatment reawakened the spirit of protest in me and I began to write again. Claire Short, then the MP for North Birmingham, took up my case but she met the same wall of silence as me. I wrote to all the influential people I had met over the last few years who had any knowledge or involvement with the penal system but not one of them was able to get to the bottom of my case.

To this day, I have received no explanation as to why I was hauled back to jail. I wasn't convicted of anything and I didn't break the conditions of my parole but I cannot afford to be bitter. Bitterness used to make me angry and violent and, when I am like that, I am my own worst enemy. If I hadn't gone back to jail, I would have still been involved with Deano and that would have only landed me back inside for even longer. During that nineteen month stretch, I had had the chance to reflect on my life and to decide what I really wanted to do on the outside and plan ahead.

On the tenth of December, 1996, I was released from Morten Hall Prison. I was forty-three years old but only sixteen of my years had been lived in freedom. The life of a gangster no longer held any appeal. In the Special Unit, I had discovered talents I never realised I had. For the short time that I was there, I made a difference and actually helped people, which was a new and satisfying experience for me. Against all the odds, I had become a role model, a shining example of rehabilitation in prisons and that brought with it a responsibility. If I failed, everyone, from my mates in Doncaster to the governors of the prisons I had been in, would have been able to claim that they had predicted my inevitable downfall. I had to prove them wrong and, as before, this filled me with the determination to succeed.

Besides, I just wasn't cut out for it anymore and it was useless to try to fit into a criminal culture that was totally different from the days when armed robbers, like myself, were at the top of the tree. Drugs were now what crime revolved around and dealing had never been something I wanted to get involved in. I didn't kid myself that it was going to be easy but twenty-seven years behind bars is enough for anyone.

I have now been out of prison for almost two years and I have found it very difficult to adapt to a conventional, domestic lifestyle beyond the prison walls. I have lived at some twenty-seven different addresses, with nine different partners, most of whom I have driven out of my life due to my complex and and frankly, damaged personality.

I have struggled to contend with persecution by both the police and the public for my past misdemeanours. Repeatedly, I have met with prejudice in my search for jobs and have experienced poverty in the many periods of unemployment between working as a journalist, lecturer and sculptor. As well as travelling widely all over Europe and various other parts of the world, I have also spoken alongside directors of prisons, church leaders, academics, three Home Secretaries, lords and even royalty, on a variety of issues surrounding crime and penal structures, in my quest to raise social awareness.

On a personal level, I have received immeasurable, on-going, support from New Bridge, as well as from my physician, Dr Marsh. I have also found a loyal ally in my old friend Mark Leech – author of the book 'Product of the System' and chairman of the newly-formed National Association of Ex-Offenders (UNLOCK). This is a unique organisation founded by three ex-offenders: Stephen Fry (actor), Bob Turney (probation officer) and Mark Leech (author). Each of them has, in his own way, successfully rebuilt his life after serving a prison sentence. They have all experienced the great difficulties faced by ex-offenders who genuinely want to go straight.

I am now living happily with my new partner, in the South of England, working on my writing and sculpting. Escaping from the clinging fog of Doncaster, which often blurred my sense of direction in the past, has stoked my enthusiasm and zest for penal reform and personal fulfillment. I fervently hope that my quest for love, security, stability and direction, is finally over.

Postscript by Dr David Wilson

I first met Frank Cook at a power-sharing conference held at HMP Grendon in the late 1980s. Frank's reputation for violence preceded him but I remember thinking, as I was being introduced to him and we started to talk for the first time, that what he said seemed to make a lot of sense. It certainly made more sense than the speech by Kenneth Baker, the then Home Secretary, who had spoken just before I met Frank, with all his political certainties about who commits crime and how we should respond. But would I, as a Prison Governor, want to share power with Frank Cook? After all, first and foremost, he was a prisoner and bureaucratic hierarchies like HM Prison Service do not take kindly to ideas of consensus, or attempts to find common ground between staff and prisoners.

Not only that, Frank was a difficult and violent man, who had beaten, slashed, kicked, rioted, taken hostages and generally done his utmost to undermine all those things that worked to maintain order in a prison. He was known to hate staff and had openly admitted that he would like to kill someone, preferably a governor. Not exactly your ideal conference delegate. The fact that he was at Grendon at all, was a testament to the fine work that was being done with Frank at the Special Unit in HMP Hull – known by the initials of the committee, the CRC (Control Review Committee) which managed allocations into the unit – and Frank's own willingness to engage in the regime. Frank clearly wanted something better than the hand that had been dealt to him and to make something of his life. Now, here he was, standing before me, chatting away twenty to the dozen and being charming and funny. I always learned that in prison it was best to expect the unexpected.

Are criminals born or made?

Few who have read the opening chapters of this book would deny the appalling circumstances of Frank's childhood. Sexually abused by his father, often abandoned with no food and inadequate clothing, illiterate and constantly beaten in an environment where violence was the norm, is it any wonder that he developed the personality that he did? Put into a children's home when his father disappeared and his mother had begun her steady decline into mental illness, he found no solace or comfort, merely an institutionalised form of what he had so far experienced in his own family. The beatings continued, only this time, the Dickensian Mrs McCabe, who ran Stanley House, administered them. Why is it that those institutions which are supposed to care for children, often seem intent on making matters worse?

Frank fared no better at school, where he was labelled 'maladjusted', distrusted by the teachers and put into the 'dunces' class'. We are only now beginning to appreciate the links between failure at school and criminality but, as we learn of Frank's school days, each incident described seems like just another episode in a life already being judged as worthless and destined for prison, rather than a career and a family. Always the gypsy outsider and unable to read or write, he found a curious acceptance in being tougher than anyone else at school – a model for living he was to adopt during his time inside. And Frank has indeed spent some time inside! Released from HMP Morton Hall in December 1996, at the age of 43, Frank had spent all but 16 years of his life in some form of institution.

Frank has experienced almost every type of incarceration. The early chapters reveal the realities of Approved Schools, Detention Centres, and Borstal – where he advises us that this was "where Frank Cook the dangerous criminal was born" and the later chapters describe life in large, Victorian local prisons, such as Strangeways in Manchester and Walton in Liverpool. They also tell us a great deal about life in our dispersal system – established in the mid 1960s to disperse notorious prisoners, or possible escape risks, around a small number of high security jails, such as Parkhurst on the Isle of Wight, or Wakefield, which Frank reminds us is situated in the ironically-named street, Love Lane. These chapters describe the reality of having to survive inside: the paranoia of having to always watch your back, routine violence, including murder, the manipulation and mind games of staff and fellow prisoners, of prison hooch and drug addiction and of situational homosexuality and rape. They are an invaluable account of the realities of an inmate sub-culture, which is often acknowledged but rarely described. Above all, Frank's story is a remarkable testimony in support of two forms of positive custody, one of which has now been undermined and destroyed and the other which has to constantly fight for its survival.

Special Units and HMP Grendon

Special Units, or CRCs, as I have described above – were established in the mid-1970s to accommodate a small but growing number of disruptive prisoners, who could not be safely housed in the mainstream prison system. By and large, the prisoners who ended up in a Special Unit were males, under forty, often sentenced to life imprisonment and usually with a long history of violence. There were three such units, situated at Lincoln, Hull and on the C Wing at Parkhurst, which largely catered for prisoners with severe psychological problems. Frank ended up in HMP Hull's Special Unit and he provides the first-ever account of what life was like in such a unit. Indeed, in much the same way as we can use Jimmy Boyle's 'A Sense of Freedom' as a source document for the Special Unit at HMP Barlinnie in Glasgow – which has since been closed – so we can read Frank's autobiography about Special Units in England and Wales.

What made Special Units 'special', was their willingness to deal with very violent prisoners in a positive or therapeutic way. Unlike the traditional approach to a violent prisoner which, by and large, involved the prison authorities being violent in return, staff in a Special Unit were encouraged to get to know the prisoners and help them to come to terms with their sentences through activities such as art, education, or music. Inevitably, this involved dealing with the prisoner as an equal, who deserved respect, rather than criticism or censure. Of course, this didn't just go one way and prisoners too had to learn to deal with staff in ways that would have been unheard of in the dispersal system. I know myself how difficult all of this could be, as I eventually ran the Special Unit at HMP Woodhill in Milton Keynes, which was set up in the early 1990s to replace Lincoln's Special Unit.

It is against this background that we should try to understand the unique and challenging nature of the regime at Hull's Special Unit, where Frank began his sculpture and gradually adopted a different outlook from the one that had characterised his approach earlier in his sentence. We should note how he came to regard staff members as friends, rather than enemies and vice versa and how this, in turn, worked to forge new loyalties and inter-relationships based on trust and respect, rather than on the prison code of mutual antipathy and hostility between staff and prisoners. If Borstal had turned Frank into "a dangerous criminal", he describes the Special Unit as helping him to change his life, proving that "even the most 'evil' men in society do have some good in them". Isn't this a powerful affirmation of this type of regime?

Unfortunately, Special Units found little favour amongst politicians, who wanted 'decent but austere' conditions inside and who thought that the way to control the prison population was to have prisoners earn privileges through an incentive scheme. Can you imagine Frank and those prisoners he describes, responding to this type of analysis? Yet, often with the collusion of staff, who didn't want 'the worst prisoners to get the best things', Special Units were closed and American-inspired ideas of 'lock down' and 'Super-maximum facilities', were imported into our own system, to cope with the likes of Frank. Indeed, the unit that I helped set up at HMP Woodhill is now a Close Supervision Centre. As I write, the prisoners in this centre are on a dirty protest, locked in their cells for twenty-three hours a day; a member of staff has been stabbed and three of the prisoners have taken the Prison Governor to the High Court, to challenge the legal basis on which they are being held in custody. Such is the price to be paid for attempting to apply simplistic, political slogans to the internal running of our prisons.

Although the Special Units have closed, HMP Grendon lives on. Indeed, there are now plans to open a wing at one of the new private prisons on the same principles that operate at Grendon. Opened in 1963 as a therapeutic community, it has long been the best thing in the Prison Service. Over the years, it has helped countless prisoners to come to terms with their offending and find the skills to develop a new, crime-free lifestyle. Frank describes his time at Grendon when the second Medical Superintendent, Ray Gillett, governed the prison. As far as I am aware and despite a growing literature about Grendon, this is the first occasion that someone who experienced it at this time has written about what it. Interestingly, Frank also describes the circumstances by which he came to be given individual therapy by Dr Gillett, as opposed to the group therapy which was the norm.

The Politics of Law and Order

HMP Grendon is always being threatened with closure, or at least seems to sit uncomfortably within the prevailing ethos of crime and punishment in this country, despite recent encouraging signs to the contrary. After all, the politics of law and order seem to suggest that crime is a choice exercised by the criminal and therefore, that the way to respond to the threat of people making that choice, is to increase the risk of detection and punish those who are caught more severely. Within this ethos, there is very little room to look at the type of people who commit crime and thus try to understand the social or economic factors that might encourage criminality. Rather, everyone is an equal player, no matter his or her class, colour, or personal circumstances. Consequently, the criminal can be held responsible for his actions and punished accordingly and thus, the government of the day can be seen to be doing something about crime.

Grendon is also about responsibility but it goes further and tries to help the prisoner make sense of his life, to see how his criminal behaviour has been shaped by the circumstances of his childhood and the relationships that he has developed, both as a child and as an adult. Here, responsibility is linked to an individual's reality, rather than a slogan to be applied as justification for punishment. This type of therapeutic intervention is costly, given that specialist staff have to be employed and other staff given specific training in order to work in this type of regime. As a consequence, the prison tries to justify its existence by publishing research demonstrating the effectiveness of its approach in relation to recidivism rates – the number of people who are released from prison only to come back again – and by inviting influential people to the prison to see it in operation. Indeed, that's why Kenneth Baker was invited to the power-sharing conference.

He and his government may have come and gone, but New Labour's approach to law and order has not, so far, differed markedly from that adopted by the Tories. The Crime and Disorder Act, for example, which became law in October 1998, has introduced parental responsibility orders, anti-social behaviour orders, local child curfews and abolished the ancient legal presumption that children were *doli incapax* (incapable of committing a wrong). All of these will serve to increase, rather than reduce, the numbers of people, especially young people, imprisoned in this country. We have also seen the extension of prison privatisation, which will create a powerful lobby of people whose financial interests are best served by the prison population increasing, rather than being reduced. Perhaps that's why we currently have over 66,000 people incarcerated in this country, our highest-ever prison population.

What does Frank's book tell us about crime, punishment and the root causes of criminality? Does it suggest that parental responsibility orders, curfews, or anti-social behaviour orders would have helped steer him away from a path of crime, and violence? Or does it instead throw light onto the inevitable failure of this type of approach when it is asked to cope with parents like Frank's and the realities of acute, gut-wrenching poverty? What does he tell us about prison and those regimes that are likely to help, rather than further stigmatise prisoners? These are decisions which you will have to make for yourself but I have no doubt that reading this book will have profoundly affected your understanding of these questions and of how to answer them.

I spoke to Frank at the conference for no more than five minutes, then we parted and I got on with being a Prison Governor. I never governed a prison that Frank was in and the next time we met was at Prison Service College in Aberford Road in Wakefield which, at the time, I ran as Head of Prison Officer and Operational Training for HM Prison Service. Peter Lee-Wright, a television producer, who would later direct us in a Channel 4 documentary called 'Hard Cell', accompanied Frank. As part of the programme, we spent several weeks together, including a wonderful trip to Slovenia, where all the prisons operate as therapeutic communities. I believe that I got to know Frank well and, despite the differences of backgrounds and experiences, what I hope that the documentary showed, was that we had far more that connected us than drove us apart. It was also clear that Frank, who had been out of prison for only a matter of months, was still trying to adjust to a life outside and stay clear of trouble. That he has so far succeeded is to his very great credit and in no small measure a testament to his personal courage and determination to leave crime behind. It is no easy matter to be an ex-prisoner and, as he describes, relationships suffer when jobs become impossible to find. Think of this, and then remember that all but 50 of the current 66,000 people we imprison will some day be released from custody.

This book is a powerful reminder that prison is an investment in failure. Not only is it costly in the conventional sense – on average it costs £25,000 to keep someone in custody for a year – but it is also costly in that its presence serves to undermine any attempt to think that there might be other ways of dealing with offenders. Unfortunately, prison is still the great Victorian institution which, even as we approach the Millennium, we seem unable to contemplate a future without. I hope that Frank's book might encourage a new debate about our prison system and, at the very least, cast some light onto places that have previously been shrouded in darkness. It deserves to be read widely.

Dr David Wilson was a prison governor from 1984 until his resignation in 1997. He worked in a variety of prisons including HMP Wormwood Scrubs, Grendon, Woodhill, HMYOI Huntercombe and Finnamore Wood and, latterly, as Head of Prison Officer and Operational Training for England and Wales. Since his resignatio, he has worked as the Senior Policy Advisor to the Prison Reform Trust and is now Senior Academic at the University of Central England in Birmingham. Dr Wilson has written widely on crime and punishment and has presented a variety of radio and television documentaries.